Self-Regulation in Learning

Self-Regulation in Learning

*The Role of Language and
Formative Assessment*

Alison L. Bailey
Margaret Heritage

HARVARD EDUCATION PRESS
CAMBRIDGE, MASSACHUSETTS

Paperback ISBN 978-1-68253-167-9
Library Edition ISBN 978-1-68253-168-6

Library of Congress Cataloging-in-Publication Data

Names: Bailey, Alison L., author. | Heritage, Margaret, author.
Title: Self-regulation in learning : the role of language and formative
   assessment / Alison L. Bailey, Margaret Heritage.
Description: Cambridge, Massachusetts : Harvard Education Press, 2018. |
   Includes bibliographical references and index.
Identifiers: LCCN 2017055586| ISBN 9781682531679 (pbk.) | ISBN 9781682531686
   (library edition)
Subjects: LCSH: Student-centered learning. | Evaluation. | Active learning. |
   Children—Language. | Teacher-student relationships.
Classification: LCC LB3051 .B24 2018 | DDC 371.39/4—dc23
LC record available at https://lccn.loc.gov/2017055586

Published by Harvard Education Press,
an imprint of the Harvard Education Publishing Group

Harvard Education Press
8 Story Street
Cambridge, MA 02138

Cover Design: Endpaper Studio
Cover Image: FatCamera/E+/Getty Images

The typefaces used in this book are Minion Pro and Myriad Pro.

For our extraordinary teachers,
Gabriella Cardenas and Olivia Lozano

Contents

Foreword

Student learning in school settings has two fundamental goals. First, students should acquire knowledge and skills in each area of the curriculum (language, mathematics, science, etc.) needed for further education, for entering the workplace, and for civic participation. Second, students should understand what it means to be a learner, how to formulate strategies and reflect on outcomes, how to use resources and collaborate with others to learn. This second goal, the self-regulation, socially shared regulation, and coregulation of learning, refers to processes that orient and motivate future learning, inside or outside school. In *Self-Regulation in Learning*, Alison Bailey and Margaret Heritage examine the first goal with a focus on language learning, but their overarching concern is with the second goal: regulation of learning in classrooms.

Bailey and Heritage take a fresh look at important elements of these goals:

- Various ways students learn (through self-regulation, socially shared regulation, coregulation)
- Language as a resource for these processes, and language development as an outcome
- Formative assessment practices designed to support the regulation of learning and to help students discover what learning to learn means

The book begins with an overview in chapter 1, "The Essentials: Putting Regulatory Processes, Language Learning, and Formative Assessment Together." In this chapter, Bailey and Heritage examine the processes of regulation and show, through concrete examples of classroom interactions, how they are linked to language learning and formative assessment. The next chapters focus successively on each type of regulation: chapter 2 on self-regulation, chapter 3 on socially shared regulation, and chapter 4 on coregulation. The final chapter discusses how classroom practices must be transformed to ensure the integration of these processes.

The examples presented in chapters 2, 3, and 4 highlight key features of each process of regulation but also show that all three processes act synergistically in classrooms. When students learn on their own (self-regulation) or learn through collaboration (socially shared regulation), various aspects of teacher-guided coregulation are simultaneously present: teachers structure the learning tasks, provide tools, define goals, ask questions, and give feedback. For example, in chapter 2, when Alan reflects on his response to a fraction problem, his self-regulatory behavior takes into account both the line of questioning of the teacher and the answers proposed by other students. In chapter 3, when Sophie, Gael, and Julie discuss possible revisions of their graphic novel, their discussion is shaped by the way the teacher sets up the task (each student group receives feedback from another group) and by the teacher's question: "What do you have to do to take the story to the next level?" At the same time, coregulation and socially shared regulation do not function independently of self-regulation; they incorporate aspects of individual self-regulation. For example, in Ms. Garcia's interaction with Aidan (chapter 4), she bases her advice on Aidan's self-monitoring: "You want to check on this one? . . . Your answer might be right. And I'm not saying it's wrong. It's always good to go back and check." The exchanges between Sophie, Gael, and Julie (chapter 3) show that their shared regulation (expressed by their use of the term *we*) draws on proposals reflecting individual self-regulation (appraisals by each student as to the best way to adjust the text: for Sophie, "make the story more fluid"; for Gael, "just add more subtle details"). In summary, educators clearly need to integrate self-regulation, socially shared regulation, and coregulation, as discussed and illustrated in chapter 5, to foster learning to learn in today's classrooms.

In addition to the many concrete examples of learning activities, classroom interactions, and formative assessments presented in each chapter, Bailey and Heritage provide, at the end of chapters 2, 3, and 4, questions and suggestions for teachers to consider and resources for observing regulatory processes in the classroom. In chapter 5, they also make recommendations for school leaders and teacher educators.

Self-Regulation in Learning emphasizes English learners. These students, for whom English—the language of instruction—is not their native or home language, are often designated in the United States as *English language learners* or, in the United Kingdom, as *learners of English as an additional language*. Many of the examples in the book concern these students, and suggestions are presented for teachers who work with them. Although the specific needs of these students should be recognized, students whose native or home language *is* English encounter many similar challenges when learning to read, write, and use English to learn other subjects. The observations, analyses, and proposals that Bailey and Heritage present are thus relevant for a wide range of students and teachers in K–12 classrooms.

This book synthesizes the results of contemporary research on student learning and incorporates the authors' direct experience of collaboration with classroom teachers. Its analyses and proposals will be of interest to classroom teachers, teacher candidates, teacher educators, and professional learning providers, as well as school administrators who wish to develop self-regulation, socially shared regulation, and coregulation in their schools and districts. Educational researchers and graduate students will also find a wealth of ideas that can stimulate new directions of research on classroom learning.

This book is a call to action for us all!

Linda Allal
Professor Emeritus
University of Geneva, Switzerland

Preface

There is a large gap in the education world when it comes to understanding how students acquire the abilities to regulate their own learning, which is key to becoming a lifelong learner, as well as assist and be assisted by others to regulate learning. As a consequence, teachers have few resources that can help them understand the mutually reinforcing relationship between these regulatory processes and students' language development and apply that knowledge in their classrooms.

In this book, we describe self-regulation and shared regulatory processes and show how they rely on a robust linguistic repertoire and, in turn, contribute to language learning. Through practical examples, we will show how teachers can help students in acquiring the language and skills to regulate their own learning. In particular, we argue that these processes can best be supported in a classroom organized around the key principles of formative assessment. In formative assessment, students understand the goals of their own learning, which is continuously monitored through self-assessment and other feedback.

Because of the close connection between these learning processes and language, the approach outlined in this book is of particular relevance for teachers of English learners. All students can develop the regulatory processes and the associated behaviors and dispositions that we describe in this book. We reject outright the notions that some students, particularly students from poor families and students who are English learners, lack some necessary qualities, background, or motivation to self-regulate, regulate the learning of others, and be regulated by teachers and peers. This book applies to *all* students, not just a privileged few, because each student must develop the necessary skills for success in college, careers, and life. However, the book will be particularly pertinent to teachers of English learners. These students would benefit from the greater degree of autonomy that regulatory processes can provide as they face the dual challenge of acquiring English and new content. Students can take charge, bringing efficiency and agency to their language and content learning.

We are grateful to Harvard Education Press for the opportunity to write this book. *Self-Regulation in Learning* brings to fruition may years of our joint thinking and interests. While writing the book, we ourselves have used self-regulation, socially shared regulation, and coregulation to grapple with sometimes-hard-to-grasp ideas and to analyze classroom practices to bring these ideas to life. We have greatly enjoyed ourselves and have had the added bonus of learning a lot along the way.

We are proud to dedicate this book to two extraordinary teachers, Gabriella Cardenas and Olivia Lozano. They have been our teachers for many years, showing us what exemplary practices in the areas we focus on look like and helping us understand what it takes to put them into practice. We have seen the results among their students, whether they are from Skid Row or more affluent areas of Los Angeles, and the results are remarkable. We owe them both an immense debt of gratitude.

Incorporating regulatory learning processes into classroom practice will require some transformations in how many teachers do business day-by-day. In this book, we offer a vision for transformative practice through real classroom examples and testimonies from students. We hope that these examples will be a source of inspiration for teachers to undertake the changes needed for students' regulation in learning. We firmly believe that if they do, the payoffs to them and their students will be worth their investment of time and energy.

Now let's get started!

CHAPTER ONE

The Essentials

Putting Regulatory Processes, Language Learning, and Formative Assessment Together

> *I think that [feedback] is very applicable to our real lives because after we graduate from high school and go to college and get a job, we [can] change what we do. By doing these things like revisions, we are able to objectively look at what we've done and learn what we need to do better and then change it so it can be better in the future. What we produce is not something that is unchangeable. I just feel like that's very applicable in real life because that's kind of how it works.*
>
> —ELEVENTH-GRADE STUDENT

Our students are growing up in a fast-changing world. No longer can we assume that the knowledge they acquire in school will equip them for life and work beyond their years of schooling. In addition to meeting the academic content requirements of college- and career-ready standards, students need to develop other critical competencies, so that they can participate in their education and pursue lifelong and life-wide learning in the dynamic future that awaits them.[1] Central among these competencies are self-regulation and shared regulation. Individual students use self-regulation to achieve academic goals, while socially shared regulation occurs in collaboration with others to meet joint academic goals.

This book examines students' regulatory processes during learning. Students develop these capacities within classroom communities of practice in which children take responsibility for their own learning as well as that of their peers. We show how a combination of these processes—self-regulation, socially shared regulation and coregulation—enable students to be successful in school. We also focus on the important role of language in these regulatory processes, which in turn serve to support the development of language.[2] Throughout the book, therefore, we pay particular attention to the students who may gain much when teachers help them self-regulate their learning—English learners. Because language skills and learning regulation are closely interrelated, efforts that support both these abilities in tandem may be especially helpful to students who are acquiring English alongside another language.[3] In schools, this language development occurs as students are also expected to acquire academic content knowledge. Additionally, we consider the significance of formative assessment as a way for teachers to enable self-regulation and socially shared regulation and as a means for students to be actively involved in assessment. We aim to help teachers help their students become self-regulated learners who can also collaborate with other students. The quote from a high school student that begins this chapter illustrates a core goal of academic self-regulation: the ability to evaluate one's own learning, decide on a path or strategy to move forward, and then take steps to make the desired improvements.

Why is self-regulation so highly prized in the classroom? In addition to its most immediate impact on a well-run, largely autonomous, and highly motivating classroom environment, students who are self-regulated learners do better in mathematics and, to a lesser degree, also in literacy and vocabulary knowledge.[4] In the case of mathematics, early self-regulation abilities predict growth in, and later attainment of, mathematics skills.[5]

Self-regulation and socially shared regulation are assisted by coregulation, the mechanism by which teachers and peers provide temporary support for acquiring self-regulatory and socially shared regulatory processes. We will focus on the synergy between language and regulated learning, the role of language in acquiring and sustaining regulatory processes, the role of regulatory processes in successful language acquisition, and how teachers can support each role in the service of the other.

In figure 1.1, we show the connections between each of the three types of regulation and language development. In addition, the figure shows the connections between coregulation and each of the two main regulatory processes (self-regulation and socially shared regulation) that are central to teaching practices and student learning—connections that we highlight in this book.

As you can see, the one-directional arrows indicate that coregulation influences the development of both self-regulation and shared regulation, and the double-headed arrows show the reciprocal influences between language and all three forms of regulation. Language is necessary both for learning and for communicating learning to others.[6] Primarily through verbal and written interactions between teachers and students and among students, individuals create knowledge and then convey it to others.[7] However, the ability to communicate your own knowledge to others is not sufficient for

FIGURE 1.1 Connections between three regulation types and the reciprocal role of language

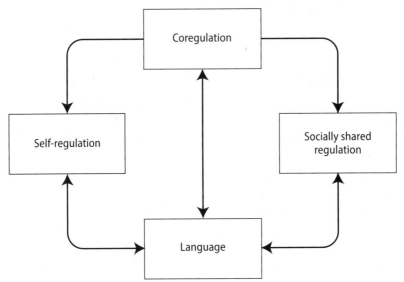

participating in collaborative learning activities in the classroom. Socially shared regulation that ensures collaboration among students requires different kinds of linguistic competencies, so that students can fully participate in, contribute to, and learn from the ongoing dialogue with others. For example, discourse skills, such as attentive listening, turn taking, soliciting clarification, probing others for knowledge, counterarguing, building on other's comments, and personal persuasion, are all invoked during any collaboration in life. Regulatory processes, therefore, rely on language and, in turn, can contribute to language learning just as they contribute to learning in other disciplines, such as reading, writing, algebra, physics, and history.

Throughout the book, we illustrate what the three regulatory processes look and sound like in action, and we show how they are made possible through language and interaction. All the examples in the book come from video or audio examples of actual classroom practice and from interviews with students. Our analyses of these examples and our recommendations are informed by the burgeoning research on regulatory processes and classroom interactions. We summarize this research throughout the book, and the classroom examples we provide underscore and expand on this research. Unless otherwise specified, the examples we present from videos and interviews come from our own collections.

Organization of the Book

In this book, we will describe many aspects of self-regulation and language learning:

- Current research, theory, and practice about self-regulation and socially shared regulation and how coregulation supports the development of both
- How college- and career-ready standards emphasize attention to students' regulatory processes
- How language is required for regulatory processes (both teaching these processes and using them in practice)
- The role of language as a source of evidence in formative assessment
- How formative assessment both promotes and relies on self-regulation, coregulation, and socially shared regulation
- How regulatory processes and language are intertwined
- The individual differences in both language learning and regulatory processes, particularly the needs of English learners

- The knowledge and skills that teachers need to support self-regulation and socially shared regulation and to use them for effective learning and assessment
- How schools and classrooms must transform to promote regulatory processes within communities of practice

After this introductory chapter, chapter 2 elaborates on the idea of self-regulation and its importance for learning. It also considers self-efficacy as a key factor in self-regulated learning and looks at what motivates self-efficacy beliefs. Given the bidirectional nature of language and self-regulation, we also discuss in detail how self-regulation can promote language learning.

In chapter 3, we turn to language learning and socially shared regulation. We examine how participation in a dyad or within a larger group can promote language learning, as well as how interactions with others can, in turn, support the development of socially shared regulation. We provide classroom examples of the benefits of shared regulation. We also pay special attention to the unique needs of English learners.

Chapter 4 looks at the role of language in coregulation. It includes examples of coregulation between teachers and students and among students as both a support for learning and evidence of the students' status in formative assessment.

Chapter 5 focuses on the integration of all three types of regulation. We address the knowledge and skills that teachers need to transform their classrooms to make these regulatory processes a consistent feature of teaching and learning. We also present ideas about how teachers can be supported to make these transformations.

A wide range of educators will find value in this book: candidate teachers and their instructors in teacher education programs; practicing teachers, both new and veteran; and administrators and anyone else in the system whose primary role is to support teachers. If you are committed to ensuring that students are ready for colleges and careers and have acquired the skills of learning how to learn for future success, then read on.

How the Three Regulatory Processes Fit into Learning

Figure 1.2 shows how the three regulatory processes for learning fit within one regulatory learning system. These can be divided into processes that regulate the behaviors of the individual student working alone (self-regulation) and those that regulate behaviors of the individual working

FIGURE 1.2   Overview of the regulatory learning system

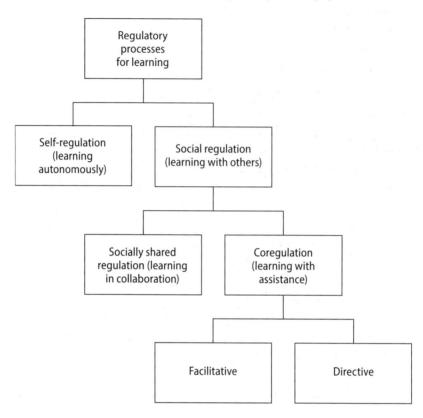

with others, either in pairs or a larger group (social regulation). Social regulation includes both socially shared regulation—the behaviors and dispositions of the individual who is collaborating with others on a joint goal—and coregulation (also referred to as *other regulation* by some authors). In coregulation, teachers, peers, and others are temporarily supporting the learning experiences of a student. Coregulation has two forms. It may be *facilitative* in focus and in outcome; that is, it assists a student who is en route to independent learning. Or it may be more *directive*; it may lead to the completion of an immediate task but may not promote student autonomy.[8] Now let's continue with more detailed descriptions of the three forms of regulatory processes.

Self-Regulatory Processes

While scholars have various concepts of self-regulation, most researchers agree that self-regulation enables learners to proactively orient their behaviors to achieving goals.[9] In this book, we focus on self-regulation in academic settings (i.e., classrooms) rather than on the management of behavior and emotions more generally, which also often comes under the self-regulation umbrella. Students who self-regulate use strategies such as setting and planning for goals, monitoring progress toward goals, and, upon reflection, adapting learning approaches to move closer to desired goals.[10] Table 1.1 describes the behaviors and dispositions related to these strategies. Table 1.2 outlines the dispositions for self-regulation and their associated characteristics. These same regulatory behaviors and dispositions occur in collaborative situations, which we will also illustrate later in the chapter.

An Example of Self-Regulation in the Classroom

This example comes from Ms. Garcia's combined first- and second-grade classroom and occurs during a lesson that is part of a unit on decomposing and composing numbers (i.e., breaking down and regrouping numbers into units, tens, and hundreds) to develop the students' understanding of place-value. Ms. Garcia organizes the mathematics lesson as a workshop that has a consistent, predictable structure. The workshop begins with an active engagement, which in this lesson is skip-counting. After posting a large piece of paper on the whiteboard with a series of numbers written on it, she invites the students to skip-count in unison by twos, then fives, and, finally, tens. Ms. Garcia then invites the students to look for patterns they see in the numbers, and she circles the patterns they identify. Next is a mini-lesson focused on composing and decomposing the number 237. After this, the students move to stations where they engage in different learning activities while Ms. Garcia conferences with individual students to formatively assess their understanding. In the final section of the lesson, a plenary session, the students reflect on their learning all together.

In the example that we'll now examine, the students are at their work stations. Some children are working alone. The others are working either with another student or in a small group or individually with Ms. Garcia.

Notice two behaviors in this example:

TABLE 1.1 Self-regulatory strategies and related behaviors and dispositions

Strategy	*Behaviors and dispositions*
Goal setting	Basing short-term goals for learning on evidence and feedback; setting and prioritizing goals and subgoals
Planning	Establishing strategies for achieving the goals; determining how much time and resources are need to achieve the goals
Self-motivation	Independently (i.e., without external rewards) using one or more strategies to keep learning on track to meeting the goals
Attention control	Attending to tasks and removing distractions from the environment; choosing conditions that make learning easier
Flexible use of strategies	Implementing multiple learning strategies across tasks and adjusting those strategies when needed to secure progress; using evidence to adapt and invent learning strategies
Self-monitoring	Monitoring progress toward learning goals and making adaptations to secure progress
Help-seeking and feedback	Seeking advice and support from adults and peers; seeking information (e.g., libraries, Internet, contacts); soliciting progress feedback from teacher and peers
Self-evaluation	Evaluating learning, independent of teachers, and making adjustment for similar tasks in the future

Source: Created in part from information found in S. Zumbrum, J. Tadlock, and E. D. Roberts, *Encouraging Self-Regulation in the Classroom A Review of the Literature* (Richmond: Metropolitan Educational Research Consortium (MERC), Virginia Commonwealth University, 2011).

- How Sarah engages in self-regulatory behavior in response to Lucy's interruption
- Sarah's use of self-directed speech

These are students at a station where the task engages them in skip-counting. Each student in their group has a piece of paper with the following written on it:

Skip-Counting and Working with Challenging Numbers and Patterns

Start at number ___. (students select a number that they choose to focus on):

- Count by 2s, 3s, 5s, or 10s.
- Record the numbers.
- Use colored pencils to show patterns you see in the numbers you record.
- Share your work with a partner at your station.

Sarah is counting aloud and then writing the numbers on her paper when Lucy leans across the table and interrupts her with an exhortation to count the next number. Here is part of their conversation. (For all the dialogue examples throughout the book, the annotations after the students' or teacher's comments highlight the regulation skills that the person is demonstrating.)

Sarah: Thirty-six, forty-one, forty-six and then . . .
Lucy: Count the next one! Count the next one! (points at Sarah's paper)
Sarah: Fifty-one . . .
Lucy: Fifty-seven, fifty-eight, fifty-nine, sixty . . .
Sarah: Wait! [*self-monitoring*]

Lucy's interjection may be an attempt to help Sarah, and we will be looking more closely at such actions as coregulation of another's learning (successful or not) in a later chapter. For now, we are focused on Sarah's commentary as she works to solve the mathematics task. The counting is moving too fast for Sarah. While her uttering "Wait!" may have been directed at Lucy's rapid counting, the word halts the counting process for Sarah so that she can take stock of where she is and not lose her place in the counting sequence. Lucy responds by pointing to a section of the paper.

Lucy: Here. (helps Sarah see the next place to write the number) Fifty-one, then fifty-six (continues the counting sequence). Get it now?

TABLE 1.2   Self-regulatory dispositions and their characteristics

Disposition	Characteristics
Belief that they can learn to learn	Students believe that through effort they can learn and that the ability to learn is not a static entity.
Willingness to persevere	Students are resilient and willing to tackle problems and find solutions.
Willingness to imagine new possibilities	Students are open to different perspectives; they are not rule bound in their thinking.
Desire to work interdependently	Students balance learning with others and learning independently to achieve goals; they are neither completely independent nor dependent, but rather learn interdependently.
Interest in being more knowledgeable	Students display an interest in becoming more knowledgeable about themselves as learners; they are willing to try out new approaches to learning, including reflection and self-evaluation.

Source: Created in part from information found in Simon Buckingham Shum and Ruth Deakin Crick, "Learning Dispositions and Transferable Competencies: Pedagogy, Modelling and Learning Analytics," in *Proceedings of the 2nd International Conference on Learning Analytics and Knowledge* (New York: Association for Computing Machinery [ACM]: 2012), 92–101.

Sarah: Sixty-eight, sixty-nine, seventy, seventy-one. (slowly counts off on her fingers)

Sarah continues to count aloud to herself, using her fingers to pace herself and to check that she is counting accurately. She reviews the sequence of numbers she has recorded and, judging that the last number is inaccurate, replaces it with a new number. In these instances, Sarah not only is engaged in self-monitoring when she stops to check her place in the sequence, but is flexibly using a combination of learning strategies in response to the counting challenge. Her strategies include slowing down the pace of counting, using her fingers as placeholders for the numbers she is counting, and counting aloud—a quintessential self-regulation behavior that very obviously uses language to guide actions. Using self-directed speech to self-regulate allows Sarah to coordinate her actions (using her fingers) with her cognition, her knowledge of a sequence of numbers.

Socially Shared Regulatory Processes

Socially shared regulation occurs in collaborative tasks when individually regulating students regulate themselves and others on the kinds of strategies described in table 1.1, for example, goal setting, planning for shared outcomes monitoring.[11] The students might also share motivation (rather than self-motivate) and share evaluation (instead of self-evaluate). Students must learn how to work collaboratively if they are to participate in peer discussions in their classrooms (and, indeed, in college and the workplace).

Collaborative discourse is both a means to learning and a product of learning. Learning through discourse is consistent with Lev Vygotsky's argument that all cognitive functions originate in, and must therefore be explained as products of, social interactions. He proposes that knowledge develops first on the social level and, later on, on the individual level—first between people (interpsychological) and then within the individual (intrapsychological).[12] When people collaborate, their learning is not limited to some prescribed level; as new ideas occur and are shared during joint problem solving, people's knowledge grows.[13] In other words, when students collaborate, they may actually learn more than if they were learning on their own. They also must learn to collaborate and engage in joint discourse to develop interpersonal skills—teamwork, negotiation skills, leadership, productivity, and so on—needed for school, work, and the rest of life.[14]

In the classroom examples we provide below, observe how socially shared regulatory processes are made possible through language and interaction. As you will see, dialogue is the conduit for regulatory processes.

Example of Socially Shared Regulation in the Classroom

This example from a high school English language arts class illustrates the kinds of regulatory process that elementary and middle school students can ultimately achieve.[15]

Notice two aspects of the students' behavior in this example:

+ The range of the regulatory behaviors the students engage in (identified in table 1.1)
+ How their exchanges build on one another to eventually create consensus about their next steps

Mr. Allen, the teacher, has given the three members of a small group the task of incorporating the feedback the group has previously received from their peers to revise the graphic novel the group has jointly created. The teacher takes the students through a process of setting a learning goal and then deciding what revisions will address their goal.

> **Mr. Allen:** What do you guys have to do to take the story to the next level? (then leaves group to attend to other groups)
>
> **Sam:** And for next steps, we need to add more characterization. [*goal setting*] And detail to the plot. What do you guys think? [*help seeking & feedback*]
>
> **Ellie:** Yeah, [*shared motivation*] but what about we focus on spacing out? [*goal setting*]
>
> **Sam:** Yeah! [*shared motivation*]
>
> **Ellie:** The action.
>
> **Sam:** Yeah. [*shared motivation*] It is going to be one panel per page. [*planning*] So the panels will be bigger, [*goal setting*] and the story will be easier to follow. [*shared evaluation*]
>
> **Mr. Allen:** (returns to the group) What I'd like you to do right now is jot down one overall goal for improvement that you need to focus on, and then I will be back to check up.
>
> **Leticia:** I think like the biggest point is still to break it up, like, into smaller . . . smaller frames. [*goal setting*]
>
> **Sam:** Well, we have to convert this disorganized two pages of rough work [*shared evaluation*] into a coherent and good-looking final product. [*goal setting*]

In this example, Sam initiates the selection of a learning goal by nominating some ideas of his own (to add characterization and further plot details), but he doesn't impose these on the group. Rather, he opens it up for discussion with "What do you guys think?," thus actively seeking their feedback. Ellie and Sam then mutually reinforce the motivation to continue with nominating learning goals with their enthusiastic yeahs between each other's turns. Ellie offers a counter suggestion of spacing out the action. Sam then calls a halt to this by providing the group with a concrete plan ("It is going to be one panel per page") to meet the goal of better readability for their readers. He even provides an overt evaluation or rationale for choosing this goal for the group: "The story will be easier to follow."

Leticia only joins in verbally (although she has been listening attentively to her peers) when Mr. Allen returns to direct them to jot down their overall goal to improve their graphic novel. She confirms her agreement with Ellie's idea by restating the suggestion for a different layout of the graphics. The exchange ends when Sam summarizes their collective thinking with an evaluation of the quality of their novel so far as "disorganized two pages of rough work" and the agreed-on goal of their revisions: "a coherent and good-looking final product."

Notice the role language is playing in these short interactions. Sam sets the tone for the exchange by using the pronoun *we*—a simple move, but one that signals the inclusive nature of their collaboration and it is picked up by Ellie. Only Leticia makes an *I* statement ("I think"), but this is likely used to stress her agreement with her collaborators' selection of a learning goal when she eventually verbally joins in the conversation to paraphrase Ellie's suggestion: "break it up, like, into smaller . . . smaller frames."

Rather than imposing his initial ideas, Sam uses a question formulation to elicit the ideas of his peers and then the rapid, interrupting backchannels ("Yeah!"), to show how simple language can be used by the students to motivate one another. In general, though, the students allow each other to build on each turn with well-articulated suggestions or paraphrases. A striking feature of this exchange is the students' command of the specialized vocabulary for the English language arts genre they are working in. Each student contributes to this topical lexicon with words like *characterization, detail, plot, panel, spacing,* and *frames.* Other terminology the students, particularly Sam, use suggests a strong grasp of general academic vocabulary that can be used across different disciplines. These words include *focus, convert, disorganized,* and *product.*

Next we will see how both self-regulation and socially shared regulation are further developed by the actions of a more experienced peer or a teacher. This more experienced person engages in coregulation by variously encouraging a student's experiences to help the student practice the behaviors outlined in table 1.1.

Coregulation Processes

Individuals self-regulate internally, whereas coregulation refers to "the joint influence of student self-regulation, and of regulation from other sources—teachers, peers, curriculum materials, assessment—on student learning."[16]

In this context, the focus is shifted from the behavior and thinking of individuals to that of an interacting pair or group. Thus, knowledge is public and is distributed among individuals and their environment.[17] Coregulation focuses on interactions between individuals and others and provides temporary support of self-regulation.[18]

Like shared regulation, coregulation comes from the concept of socially mediated learning and human learning as culturally based communication through which people share and build knowledge.[19] It is grounded in intersubjectivity, which involves participants in a shared focus around a common task, and scaffolding.[20]

Scaffolding, a metaphoric concept, refers to the assistance, ideally temporary, that teachers or peers provide to learners to solve a problem, carry out a task, or achieve a goal that would be beyond the learners' unassisted efforts. Scaffolding involves a range of functions. Teachers or peers can enlist the student's interest in, and adherence to, the requirements of the task (attention control; self-monitoring). They can accentuate certain relevant features of the task (goal planning), and they can make the pursuit of the particular objective meaningful enough that the student will risk the next step (self-motivation, planning, flexible learning strategies).[21] Also, scaffolding is contingent—that is, based on immediate student responses and involves the transference of responsibility from the teacher to the student.[22] When scaffolding occurs during an interaction around a task, a "shared understanding based on a common focus of attention and some shared pre-suppositions form the ground for communication."[23]

The earlier example illustrates coregulation when Lucy first points to Sarah's paper as a joint focus (intersubjectivity) and helps her see the next number in the skip-counting sequence. We'll now return to Ms. Garcia's first- and second-grade classroom to see how Ms. Garcia uses coregulation when she meets one-on-one with another student, Aidan, a first-grader, to assess his progress in solving the problem he has been set.

Example of Coregulation in Support of Self-Regulation

Notice the following aspects of coregulation in this example:

- How Ms. Garcia's responses to Aidan depend on what she hears him say
- How she scaffolds his learning rather than transferring her knowledge directly to him

This interaction shows how Ms. Garcia, as the "expert" in the situation, assists the "novice" Aidan. Ms. Garcia's actions have a pedagogical goal; her coregulation actions are in the temporary service of Aidan's own nascent self-regulated learning while he is still acquiring specific mathematical skills and knowledge. The teacher practices several coregulation behaviors by both modeling and directly referring to strategies of self-regulation for Aidan. Notice how the behaviors in table 1.1 are reflected in this exchange.

As described earlier, the students in Ms. Garcia's class are working at different stations during a section of the mathematics lesson. For one group of students at their station, Ms. Garcia has established the following learning goal and success criteria, which she has posted on frames on the students' table.

Success Criteria for One-Step Word Problems in Mathematics

Today our goal as mathematicians is to represent your understanding of a one-step word problem.

- ☐ I can unpack the word problem by identifying the action and the problem.
- ☐ I can use a math strategy or strategies to show my understanding of the problem.
- ☐ I can use necessary math tools to help me solve the problem.
- ☐ I can justify my reasoning giving a logical explanation (written and oral while also using math vocabulary).

The teacher has an initial discussion with the students about the goal and the criteria to make sure that they understand what is involved in this learning, the kind of language they will use in their explanations, and the tools that are available for problem solving. Each student has the problem on an individual sheet.

Math Problem Solving

Aidan and Kevin together have __ base-ball cards. Kevin's father gives them __ more baseball cards to add to their collection.

How many baseball cards do they have altogether?

Choose from these numbers:

(39, 16)   (724, 236)   (13, 17)

Show your work here (space was included below for students' representations).

From the options provided, the students are to select the number combinations that they think best match their level of place-value knowledge. (Ms. Garcia often offers options like these to accommodate the range of mathematical understanding in her students and to involve students in actively thinking about their own learning status.)

After spending time meeting with other children in the class, Ms. Garcia returns to this group and sits next to Aidan, who is working on his solution to the number combination (724, 236). He begins to describe his problem-solving strategy, and the following interaction between him and Ms. Garcia ensues:

Aidan: Which makes them easy to add up.

Ms. Garcia: Mmm . . . I see.

Aidan: And the way how I added the two hundred with the seven hundred is that I know that seven plus three equals ten, so seven plus two must equal nine, so seven hundred and two hundred must equal nine hundred.

Ms. Garcia: Ah. And I noticed (points at Aidan's paper) that you have fifty and a ten—right? [coregulation: *flexible learning strategy*; *attention control*]

Aidan: Yes.

Ms. Garcia: So you have five tens here and one ten here. Which? . . .

Aidan: Which makes sixty.

Ms. Garcia: Which makes sixty. So then it's taking nine hundred and grouping that with sixty to give you? . . .

Aidan: Nine hundred and sixty.

Ms. Garcia: Nine hundred and sixty. Do you think that just by looking at your strategy right now, is it tricky pulling down numbers and keeping it organized? [coregulation: *self-monitoring*]

Aidan: Um, yeah, it's a little tricky.

Ms. Garcia: Is it? Mmm. Do you think (points at Aidan's paper) you've counted all the numbers necessary to get your answer? [coregulation: *self-monitoring*]

Aidan: Well, if I got this answer on both sides (turns over his paper), then, probably, yes.

Ms. Garcia: So I'm noticing that you are also checking your work. You are going back and checking, aren't you? [coregulation: *flexible learning strategy*; *attention control*; *self-monitoring*]

Aidan: Yeah.

Ms. Garcia: Well, do you think this would be (points at Aidan's paper) the correct answer to this question? [coregulation: *self-evaluation*]

Aidan: Yes.

Ms. Garcia: What do you know about the question? What does it seem to be asking you? [coregulation: *self-evaluation*; *planning*]

Ms. Garcia models how she would use the practice of noticing as a flexible learning strategy. This modeling shows Aidan how she is carefully attending to tasks to effectively check the work when she points to his paper early in the exchange and says, "And I noticed that you have fifty and a ten—right?" Again, later on she says, "So I'm noticing that you are also checking your work. You are going back and checking, aren't you?" This second example also shows Ms. Garcia directly asking Aidan if he is self-monitoring the accuracy of his work as he goes along.

Additionally in this exchange, we see Ms. Garcia direct Aidan to self-monitor the effectiveness of his choice of mathematical approach when she asks, "Do you think that just by looking at your strategy right now, is it tricky pulling down numbers and keeping it organized?" And again, later, "Do you think (pointing at Aidan's paper) you've counted all the numbers necessary to get your answer?" This exchange is followed up by a request for Aidan to self-evaluate the accuracy of his work when she asks, "Well, do you think this would be (pointing at Aidan's paper) the correct answer to this question?" She brings Aidan back to the original goal of the mathematics problem with her final set of questions to him: "What do you know about the question? What does it seem to be asking you?" Her questions both invoke self-evaluation of his current knowledge state and require a review of how he had interpreted and planned to solve the question.

Collectively, the teacher's coregulation moves focus on both showing and telling Aidan how to pay close attention to the work he is doing along the way and to finally scrutinize for himself whether his work has resulted in an accurate response to the original mathematics question. Note that Ms. Garcia never tells Aidan if he is right or wrong. Nor does she give him the correct answer throughout the eighteen turns they take in this one interaction.

In terms of language, Ms. Garcia asks Aidan a range of questions that shift from yes-or-no tag questions (e.g., "you have fifty and a ten—right?") to questions requiring fill-in-the-blank answers ("grouping that with sixty to give you? . . .") to an open-ended question that does not assist Aidan in his response. She also draws on a wide range of topic vocabulary (e.g., *add, counted, numbers, grouping*) and general academic vocabulary that cuts across different disciplines (e.g., *noticed, strategy, organized, necessary, checking*).

The teacher's choice of verbs and verb tenses is striking and signals a quasi-collegial relationship through which Aidan is invited to offer his own interpretation of the original mathematics word problem. For example, the use of the conditional form "would be" when she points to Aidan's paper and asks, "Do you think this would be the correct answer to this question?" suggests the possibility of a counterpoint. Her last questions, "What do you know about the question? What does it seem to be asking you?," also invite Aidan's own interpretation of the intent of the word problem rather than taking the meaning at face value. Whether Aidan can engage with the deeper meaning of these questions at this young age is not evident in this interaction. But through her own use of language, Ms. Garcia has given him exposure to this nuanced way of thinking and speaking.

Coregulation in Support of Socially Shared Regulation

Coregulation need not be used only to support the self-regulation of individual students. It also helps encourage socially shared regulation. For example, when a teacher facilitates discussion of goal setting, planning, monitoring, and evaluation with groups of students, he or she is also engaging in coregulation, but this time in the service of the students' socially shared regulation. A final example, from Ms. Garcia's combined first- and second-grade mathematics lesson, illustrates how a teacher supports socially shared regulation by gathering the whole class to jointly work through the decomposition of a three-digit number.

Notice the following features of coregulation in this example:

- The nature of Ms. Garcia's questions and how they stimulate coregulation
- How she encourages students to think about novel approaches

During the mini-lesson part of the workshop, Ms. Garcia writes the number 237 on the board. She asks one student to read the number and then poses a question to the entire class: "What are a few ways I could break this number apart?" One student says, "You could have two hundreds, three tens, and seven ones." Ms. Garcia writes these groupings on the board and then invites the children to count them with her.

Ms. Garcia: What should we start with? Larry? [coregulation: *goal setting*]

Larry: The ones. (another child says no) [*shared monitoring*]

Ms. Garcia: Do you disagree with Larry? Sonia? [coregulation: *shared monitoring*]

Sonia: Ah . . . uh . . .

Ms. Garcia: Should we start with the ones? [coregulation: *goal setting*]

Sonia: I think we should start with the hundreds. [*goal setting*]

Ms. Garcia: Why should we start with the hundreds? [coregulation: *shared monitoring*]

Sonia: Because . . . uh . . . you can count the one hundreds . . . and . . . uh . . . then the ones, then equals, and then you can equal it up.

Ms. Garcia: Ah . . . so we can count up. So far we have heard that [coregulation: *shared monitoring*] we can start by counting ones. Sonia suggested we start by counting the hundreds, then the ones. Mmm, does anyone have another way, a different way, of counting them? [coregulation: *goal setting*]

Jake: Well, I'm also with Sonia for the hundreds but then the tens, and then the ones. [*goal setting*]

Ms. Garcia: Can I ask you why we would start with the hundreds and then move on to the tens? [coregulation: *shared monitoring*]

Jake: Well, it would be easier to add them up because all you need to do is . . . like . . . if there's two hundreds, then that's two hundred, if there's three tens, that's thirty, and if there's seven ones, that's going to be seven. And then you just add them all up. It's way easier than counting from the hundreds then the ones. [*shared monitoring*] Like two hundred, seven . . . it's weird . . . [*evaluation*] and then if you could by the ones, you're going to be, like, going up . . . like seven, thirty, two hundreds. (laughs)

Ms. Garcia acknowledges that there are several ways to count and suggests that, on this occasion, the students count by hundreds, tens, then ones. The children count in unison while Ms. Garcia points to the number groups in turn. But to get to this point, she has skillfully coregulated the students' setting of a shared goal by asking a series of open-ended questions (e.g., "What should we start with?," "Why should we start with the hundreds?," "Why we would start with the hundreds and then move on to the tens?"). The students respond by nominating a specific strategy for starting the counting process. To make clear that different possibilities can be entertained and deliberated on by the whole class, Ms. Garcia calls for additional novel approaches, explicitly asking, "Does anyone have another way, a different way, of counting them?" This question enables the students to both participate and hear the range of different ideas of their classmates as they discuss decomposing the three-digit number. Ms. Garcia also models ways of making a counterproposal to Larry's initial suggested goal by asking if the other students disagree. In addition, she models ways of monitoring the class's collective progress when she recaps where they are in the discussion of goal setting: "So far we have heard that we can start by counting ones." The students show regulatory moves that include goal setting, shared monitoring, and possibly even shared evaluation from Jake (a second-grader) when he dubs one of the proposed ways of counting "weird."

At the discourse level, students are expected to pay close attention to each other's responses and build on each turn in a meaningful, contingent way, as Jake does when he says, "Well, I'm also with Sonia for the hundreds." The vocabulary Ms. Garcia and the students use includes just a few specialized terms from the mathematics register—*counting* and *equals*. Instead,

Ms. Garcia and the students depend heavily on familiarity with informal, shorthand terminology like *the ones* and *the tens* to refer to the units in the three-digit target number.[24]

Ms. Garcia also adopts a discourse pattern of repeating a student's turn by incorporating it into her own turn, presumably as a check on her grasp of the student's intended meaning and also as a way of broadcasting it again for the rest of the class to contemplate before they move on to the next turn. We see this approach in the exchange with Sonia when Sonia ends her turn with, "Then the ones, then equals, and then you can equal it up," and Ms. Garcia revises this slightly with "Ah . . . so we can count up."

Regulatory processes like those used by the students and supported by Ms. Garcia allow students to organize their language learning experiences effectively, whether for communicating their ideas or learning the language necessary for productive classroom participation. In turn, well-developed language abilities are important to regulatory processes for a variety of reasons: Much of self-regulation requires internal speech to guide a learner's planning and reflection. Voicing one's own thoughts or narrating one's own actions out loud can also help guide a learner during particularly challenging problem solving because speaking out loud can slow down processing speed and buy time for the learner to organize his or her ideas and plans. Furthermore, language is obviously necessary both for the expression of ideas and knowledge and for productive participation during collaborative activities that rely on self-regulation and shared regulation. Finally, language is the medium through which coregulation—vital to the acquisition of both self-regulation and socially shared regulation—occurs.

While the regulatory processes we have described can be explained and understood separately, they occur simultaneously and in an integrated manner. Each regulatory form, however, warrants specific attention and entails specific teaching strategies, which we lay out in the different chapters of the book.

So far, we have described regulatory process and the role that language plays in their development. In the next section, we discuss language learning and how it relates to regulatory processes.

Language Learning

Language can be characterized by students' *receptive* language, which covers their listening and reading comprehension skills and how these skills are acquired. Students' need receptive language skills to obtain new content knowledge and other skills. For example, students may be required to listen to a teacher's oral explanation of the solar system and then research the information further by searching for, and reading about, the relationships between Earth and the other planets. This learning environment enables teachers to assess content learning and language skills and provide feedback, and for students to assess themselves and get peer feedback related to the goals of the task.

Students also need *productive* language, which is the language capabilities students must have to speak and write to engage with content ideas and principles and to demonstrate their new learning. For example, students discuss how they will group pennies to represent how they used multiplication to solve a mathematics problem. They later independently write about their grouping strategy so that their teacher can gauge how well they understand multiplication and the specific demands of the task.

Our view of language learning is consistent with the ideas of social constructivist or interactionist approaches to learning.[25] A social constructivist or interactionist account of language development suggests that learning is embedded in an individual's social encounters (e.g., talk at mealtimes, collaborating with classmates). Learning language is first external (social, interpersonal, and regulated by expert others) and then becomes internalized (intrapersonal and self-regulated).[26] Teachers can extend these ideas to foster regulatory processes within their classrooms. They can model new skills and uses of knowledge (language and academic content). They can also scaffold the learner's experiences through assistance well attuned to a student's needs. Finally, teachers can use routines that are helpful to language learners, especially as the learners begin to predict which expressions go with which interactions, events, or people.

Other theoretical approaches to language learning are also encountered in the research literature. Whenever they can illuminate certain cases, we also include these approaches in the book.[27]

English Learners

In each chapter, we introduce key considerations for instruction with English learners. We also discuss the variation in their language- and content-learning trajectories and the special attention and strategies teachers can adopt to address their language needs. Including this sizable and rapidly growing group of students reflects how English learners are being integrated within the general education classrooms of many educators. This burgeoning cadre of general education teachers, many of whom are teaching English learners for the first time, is now responsible for integrating English language development and English language arts and needs guidance on this challenge.[28] Our special focus also recognizes the complexity of the work conducted by English language coordinators and ESL (English as a second language) specialists. Teachers of English learners have in their classrooms students at many levels of English proficiency. These teachers stand to gain enormously from having students self-regulate their own learning. For instance, when students are self-regulated, teachers can more easily attend to the individual linguistic needs of students without losing the learning momentum of the whole class. Teachers also benefit from fostering students' socially shared regulation skills, which help the students develop language in authentic situations such as small-group collaboration on tasks structured to require oral and written participation from each student.

Deeper Learning

Noting that college- and career-ready standards are intended to promote deeper learning, a recent report from a committee of the National Research Council (NRC) identified an interplay of three broad areas of competence for deeper learning. NRC defined this interplay as "the process through which an individual becomes capable of taking what was learned in one situation and applying it to new situations (i.e., transfer)."[29] Each of the broad areas of competence—cognitive, intrapersonal, and interpersonal—includes clusters of competence (figure 1.3).

Our ideas about regulatory processes introduced in earlier sections are reflected in these deeper learning competencies. For example, self-regulation involves metacognition (i.e., thinking about one's thinking) and socially shared regulation and coregulation involve collaboration and responsibility. The convergence between regulatory processes and deeper learning competencies lends support for regulatory processes as a key goal if students are to fully develop their capacities to achieve college- and career-ready standards and become self-sustaining, lifelong learners.

FIGURE 1.3   Competencies for deeper learning

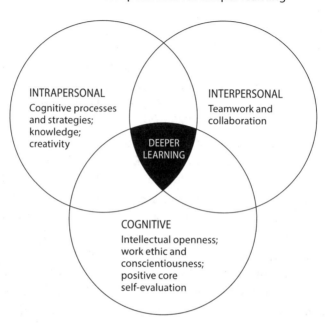

Formative Assessment and Regulatory Processes

In addition to regulatory processes and language, formative assessment, or assessment *for* learning, is integral to the teaching and learning process.[30] Assessment, which has a summative function, meaning an evaluation of what students have learned to date, presents a retrospective view of learning. In contrast, the goal of assessment *for* learning is to provide a prospective view, anticipating future possibilities in learning. The difference between these two perspectives is well captured in this observation: in addition to looking "upstream at what has been learned, assessment needs to look downstream at what can be learned."[31] This perspective expresses the essential purpose of formative assessment: to move students' learning forward while their learning is still in development.[32]

Formative assessment operates as a feedback loop in which both teachers and students play distinctive, yet complementary, roles in support of learning. The students improve their self-regulation when they are joint stakeholders in assessment with their teachers and peers. In this context, they have the right and obligation to play a significant role in analysis and reflection about their own learning and in deciding on next steps in learning based on their own self-monitoring and on feedback from their teachers and peers. In this way, they advance their learning and become self-regulated learners.

In formative assessment, the teacher establishes clear learning goals and performance criteria (success criteria). The teacher interprets evidence of learning against the criteria while the learning is continuing and makes immediate or nearly immediate adjustments to teaching and learning in the light of the evidence. Among other adjustments to teaching and learning, the teacher can provide feedback and involve the students in the assessment.[33]

During instruction, teachers intentionally elicit responses from students during the ongoing flow of activity and interactions in the classroom.[34] Teachers often use how well and often a student interacts in the classroom as evidence in their formative assessment.[35] As we have seen in the preceding examples, socially shared regulation and coregulation occur through interaction, and such interaction can provide teachers with evidence not only about students' thinking but also about language learning and the students' abilities to collaborate. Evidence gathering is planned and has a place in the rhythm of instruction; it is built in as part of the ongoing interaction between the teacher and students. Such interaction ensures that they are mutually and closely involved in a common purpose.[36]

The evidence teachers obtain helps them support the students' immediate or near-immediate next steps in learning so that learning is continuously moving forward.[37] In this way, the teachers are making contingent, evidence-based pedagogical responses to match their actions to the students' *zones of proximal development*, the term used for the metaphorical space where learning occurs.[38] In classroom learning, this zone refers to the difference between what students can do on their own and what they can do with assistance from a teacher or peer.[39] Teachers interpret the evidence of their students' learning status and decide which form of assistance they will provide to advance the students' learning. The ultimate goal is to reach the point when students internalize the learning and make it part of their own independent achievement.

In formative assessment, students self-regulate through their own self-monitoring and self-assessment and by responding to teacher and peer feedback. In accord with a prospective view of assessment, students actively monitor and assess their learning progress against established learning goals and performance criteria—prerequisites for formative assessment and then judge whether they have met or are near their goal.[40] When they perceive a discrepancy between their current status and the goal, they can take strategic action to meet that goal.[41] For example, if students feel they are not making the desired progress, they might ask for feedback, reorganize information, make connections to similar tasks they have successfully accomplished previously, or do more research. Formative assessment involves a sequence of two actions. First the learner considers the gap between a desired goal and his or her present state of knowledge, understanding, or skill, or some combination thereof. Second, the learner takes some action to close that gap between the present status and the desired goal.[42] These actions are consistent with self-regulatory processes through which students are metacognitively, motivationally, and behaviorally active participants in their own learning processes.[43]

As noted above, in addition to the internal feedback students generate in formative assessment, they receive external feedback from teachers and their peers. This feedback also provides information about the discrepancy between the students' current status and desired goals. When the feedback focuses on providing information about student performance (in relation to goals and success criteria) and provides suggestions—rather than solutions or correct answers—it is much more effective than evaluative feedback that only informs the student how well he or she is doing.[44] Moreover, feedback should not involve the ego, for example, providing praise only, and it should engage students' thinking. In terms of self-regulation, students can reflect on the feedback they receive and decide how—or even if—to use the feedback to advance their learning.

The regulatory processes we have introduced in this chapter, as well as formative assessment, occur in the contexts of classroom communities of practice, and we now turn to that topic.

Communities of Practice

The term *communities of practice* refers to the formation of groups around a common set of practices, procedures, and standards deployed in pursuit of some goal.[45] For example, a group of artisans, weavers, or carpenters forms a community of practice and communicates those practices, procedures, and standards to apprentices seeking to become artisans. The idea of classroom communities of practice was foreshadowed by philosopher and psychologist John Dewey. He proposed that learning should not be thought of as an individualized process of knowledge acquisition, because "all activity takes place in a medium, a situation, and with reference to its conditions."[46] Instead of expecting an individual to develop understanding or skills by himself or herself, as is often the case in more traditionally oriented classrooms, a community of practice recognizes that knowledge is distributed among individuals and their environment.[47]

In classroom communities of practice, students are apprentices in pursuit of the goal of learning, and to this end, they employ practices, procedures, and standards. For example, through the practice and procedures of formative assessment, teachers and students gather and act on information about each student's learning status so as to continually advance all participants' learning. In the process, the teachers help each student become effective assessors and managers of their own learning. Additionally, in communities of practice, teachers establish the norms for respectful listening and building on the ideas of others. In this vein, teachers set up structures such as worthwhile collaborative tasks that genuinely engage students in joint activity and require students to listen to each other and negotiate common solutions. These kinds of practices, procedures, and structures enable the development of self-regulation, socially shared regulation, and coregulation.

Throughout the chapters in this book, we will return to the idea of communities of practice, as we consider in detail the intersection of language and regulatory processes and the context in which they emerge and flourish. Now we move on to chapter 2, where we focus in detail on self-regulation.

CHAPTER TWO

Self-Regulation

Becoming an Effective Lifelong Learner

Sometimes I disagree with the feedback,
then I have to decide what my next steps are.

—NINTH-GRADE STUDENT

If students are first to be effective learners of language and then effective users of language in the classroom, they will need to learn to self-regulate. They must develop the requisite self-knowledge and skills to deliberately set goals for their own learning, consciously plan their time, and select meaningful tasks to achieve those goals. They must also know how well they are progressing toward their goals and whether they need to implement remedies if they are off course. From the ninth-grader's statement above, we get an insight into a self-regulated learner. This student values feedback but does not simply follow it without further reflection. He has the confidence to judge the feedback and decide for himself if he should use the feedback to improve his work or if he should take another direction. This chapter will describe in depth what self-regulated competencies entail, how students develop in these areas, and what teachers should be doing to assist students in their acquisition. We pay particular attention to how the students interact with language both as an outcome of such self-regulation and as a medium through which self-regulation is supported. We illustrate the competencies with a range of student voices taken from interviews in which students were asked about self-regulatory processes.

Self-Regulated Learners

Figure 2.1 shows where we are within the overall regulatory learning system. We start with the individual students and their behaviors and dispositions that make them self-regulated learners who view learning as an activity they do for themselves proactively rather than simply a reactive response to teaching.[1] They take a purposeful approach to learning by setting goals, developing plans to achieve those goals, monitoring progress toward the

FIGURE 2.1

Overview of the regulatory learning system: where self-regulation fits

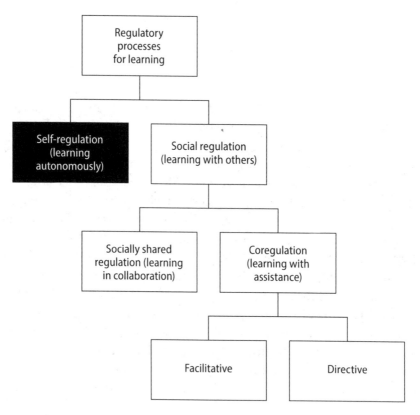

goals, and, when necessary, adapting learning approaches to move closer to desired goals.[2]

As a second-grade student observes, "it's important to have a goal 'cause if you are just trying to do something that you already know, it's not gonna really help you. But if you have a goal and you try to meet your goal, it could help you. And the success criteria [are] important also cause if you have a goal but you don't know how to meet it, then how are you supposed to get it?"

At his young age, this student already understands the value of not only goals but also success criteria to learning. Success criteria indicate what students can do if they meet their goals. This second-grader is well on the way to being a self-regulated learner.

The approaches adopted by self-regulated learners are consistent with the cognitive, interpersonal, and intrapersonal competencies of flexibility and metacognition outlined in the deeper learning framework for college and career readiness in chapter 1. Self-regulated learners are more likely to succeed academically and to view their future optimistically.[3] They are also more persistent, resourceful, and confident.[4] They have strong self-efficacy beliefs, are motivated to learn, and are metacognitive as they learn.

Belief in Self-Efficacy

Students' views of their own academic self-efficacy can influence their self-regulation in learning. Self-efficacy refers to an individual's beliefs in his or her capacity to perform actions that lead to a specific goal.[5] For instance, students who have high self-efficacy beliefs in their reading abilities are more likely to persevere with challenging texts than those with low self-efficacy beliefs in reading. In fact, students with low self-efficacy beliefs may decide they will not be successful even before they tackle the challenging text and may quickly give up. Students who have high self-efficacy beliefs work harder and persevere longer than do students who have doubts about their capabilities.[6] They are also better at monitoring and adapting their performance than are students with low-efficacy beliefs.[7]

Returning to the second-grade student quoted above, we can see that, during this interaction with his teacher, he believes in his own capabilities and understands the value of working on a task that is just right for him, neither too hard nor too easy. In the following segment, he is referring to how he thinks about the number combinations he selects for his mathematics problem (see the "Math Problem Solving" assignment in chapter 1).

Nami: I wanted to mention about what helps me pick just-right numbers: it's the picture of the person who is going down the mountain on the bike and the person who is going up the mountain on the bike and then the person who is on the just-right road.

Ms. Garcia: So we introduced that graphic when we were learning to choose just-right numbers, that's right. So what does that mean—it's a cyclist, right? What does it mean when he's going up the hill?

Nami: They're struggling on a problem, and when he goes down the hill, it means you're going super quickly and just finishing the problem and it's way too easy. But when he goes on the just-right path, it's a just-right number for you. And usually what happens is there are some ups, where it's a little hard, but then it gets easier. And then it's a little hard but it gets easier.

Nami recognizes that learning involves some challenges that can be overcome so that ultimately the learning becomes easier as knowledge and skills are consolidated.

Motivation

Self-efficacy underlies motivation; unless students believe that their actions can produce the results they desire, as our second-grade student does, they have little incentive to act or persevere when faced with difficulties.[8] Motivation offers four main advantages for self-regulated learning. First, motivated students increase their attention to their learning. Second, motivation can expand the diversity in a student's choice of task (for example, if a person is motivated to learn a musical instrument, she is more likely to choose to learn it). Third, high motivation can also increase a student's effort to learn something difficult. And finally, motivated students are more likely to persevere by persisting on a time-consuming task to achieve success.[9] These motivational factors resonate with the deeper learning competencies of conscientiousness and work ethic.

Two additional motivational factors bear on students' self-regulation abilities. First, students' commitment to, and interest in, the learning goals at hand can lead them to perceive learning as either worthwhile or not worth doing. When students see little value in a task, they do not bring the goal-oriented perspective associated with self-regulation to their learning. This point underscores the need for teachers to engage students in learning opportunities that the students perceive as relevant, have an intrinsic value to their own learning, and have a clear purpose. Second, students' affective response to learning can have an impact on motivation. For example, when students feel anxious about their learning, as they may do when asked to learn something too far removed from their current competence, they will be less likely to adopt self-regulated approaches to learning.[10]

Metacognition

Metacognition, the ability to reflect on one's own learning and to make adjustments when necessary, is a competence for deeper learning and a facet of self-regulated learning. The value of reflecting on one's learning is well summed up by this high school student: "I also think doing a self -reflection in the beginning and the end of class kind of helps you figure out where you are, and then how much you actually got from the discussion. So, for example, in the beginning of class, you really have no idea. Which was me, in the beginning of this class. But then after discussion, and after reflecting, I'm like, 'Oh, I really did learn a whole bunch of stuff. I really did get stuff from my peers!'"

Metacognition for self-regulation includes self-appraisal and self-management.[11] Self-appraisal refers to reviewing one's knowledge and cognitive strategies, as the high school student above does. When learners monitor and regulate their learning through planning and adapting learning strategies accordingly, they are self-managing.

Here, a first-grade student talks about how she engages in self-appraisal and self-management: "About self-assessment: Like, if you think you're done, don't say to yourself, 'I'm done; I'm gonna go show the teacher.' Don't say that to yourself. Say, 'Do I actually think I'm done?' Ask yourself questions: 'Do I actually think I'm done? I should probably check my work again.' Probably nine plus eight is not the answer I got, probably it's, like, something different. That's why you always have to self-assess before you show the teacher that you're done."

Self-management also includes removing distractions from a learning situation, engaging in effective time management, and applying focused effort in learning.[12]

Being metacognitive distinguishes stronger learners from less competent ones. For example, when students have metacognitive skills, they can explain the strategies they used to solve a problem and why, whereas less competent students monitor their learning sporadically and ineffectively and provide incomplete explanations.[13] Effective problem solvers have highly developed metacognitive skills. They know how to recognize flaws or gaps in their own thinking, articulate their thought processes, and revise their efforts.[14]

Because of the importance of self-regulation to deeper learning, the good news is that these capabilities are malleable and can be taught and that students' feelings of self-efficacy and motivation can be enhanced. Later in the chapter, we will consider how teachers can provide the conditions for developing self-regulation, including metacognition, self-efficacy, and motivation.

The Role of Feedback in Formative Assessment and Self-Regulation

Feedback is the centerpiece of formative assessment and the primary means through which students' self-regulatory processes are supported. Through feedback, students gain information on how their current learning status compares with the learning goals and success criteria. Students obtain feedback from external sources, such as teachers and peers, and from the internal feedback students generate as they engage in learning and self-assess their progress toward goals.[15]

A first-grader explains how she uses self-assessment to generate internal feedback: "Say I am in math and I did this whole problem, and before I go to show my problem [to the teacher], I should think about it and look at it again and maybe do another problem to see if my answer is correct, just to make sure it's correct. 'Cause you don't need someone to tell you 'Oh, it's wrong,' 'Oh, it's right.' You should self-assess before."

In a virtuous circle, the more self-regulated the students are, the more they are able to generate and use internal feedback (i.e., self-assessment) and use external feedback to achieve their goals.[16]

Concepts of Quality

Whatever its source, feedback depends on the ability of students to hold "a concept of quality that is roughly similar to that held by teacher."[17] Consequently, either at the outset of, or during, the learning episode, teachers must help their students understand what meeting the learning goals entails. For example, when students are learning to write persuasive essays, a teacher might, to clarify the learning goal, explore a strong and a weak example of persuasive writing and discuss the criteria that make an essay stronger or weaker. In mathematics, a teacher could discuss different solutions that students (not in the same class) have used to solve problems and what makes the approaches stronger or weaker.

Sometimes teachers mistakenly think that checklists are success criteria. But instead of providing students with a concept of what it means to achieve the intended learning, checklists merely become lists of items to check off, like a to-do list.[18] As a checklist of what students have to do to complete the task, the criteria do not provide a standard of quality against which students can assess their own learning. On the other hand, when students clearly understand the learning goals and success criteria, they have a standard against which they can compare their own work as they monitor their progress. They are also better able to connect external feedback they receive to the learning at hand. This connection is underscored by a fifth-grade student: "Success criteria are a useful tool; it helps me know what to look for. I follow the success criteria to give feedback to my partner."

Self-Assessment Skills: Monitor, Evaluate, Decide on Next Step

In self-assessment, students monitor and evaluate the quality of their thinking and behavior when they are learning, and they identify ways to improve their learning. It involves students in three components of a cyclical, ongoing process: (1) self-monitoring—being aware of thinking and progress as it occurs; (2) self-evaluation—identifying progress toward a goal, asking oneself, "Am I on track, or do I need to take some corrective action?"; and (3) deciding on an action to take to keep moving forward toward the goal of improvement.[19] While self-assessment is a means to generate and use internal feedback, self-assessment is also essential to using external feedback appropriately.[20] Not all feedback may be useful; students need to know this and learn to discriminate among the feedback comments they receive. As the introductory statement in this chapter showed, students need to compare the feedback they have received with their own assessment and decide how—and, indeed, if—they will use it.

If teachers are to implement self-assessment strategies, they have to see these skills as a priority, not an afterthought, consistently building them into the students' learning routines. Teachers can support self-assessment skills in many ways:

- Provide models through think-alouds, when they describe their own internal processes while they are self-assessing, including modeling how they ask self-monitoring questions (e.g., "Did I understand what I just read?," "Does this solution make sense?," "Is my point of view clear?").
- Provide structured reflection and self-assessment opportunities in the lesson with templates and protocols that are included as regular elements of a lesson. A protocol might include, for example, questions about what the student has learned, what was difficult during learning, what the student needs to spend more time learning.
- Ask students to think about their own learning with respect to goals and criteria and to decide what they would like to have feedback on to help them to move forward.
- Ask students to reflect on where they are in relation to meeting the goals and success criteria, why they think they are there, and what they might do next, depending on their own self-assessment.
- Talk with the students about their own feedback to help them understand how they judged their own learning in relation to the goals and criteria.

Using External Feedback

Good-quality external feedback has been characterized as "information that helps students trouble-shoot their own performance and self-correct: that is, it helps students take action to reduce the discrepancy between their intentions and the resulting effects."[21] In other words, the feedback teachers provide should help students to know what they are doing well in relation to the goals and criteria, and offer suggestions or cues to help them think about how they can take action that will move their learning forward.

For example, in a ninth-grade mathematics classroom, students were learning about slope and were given tasks that required them to answer the question "What is the slope of the line graphed here?" As the teacher circulated among the students to observe their work, she gave this feedback to one of the students: "Remember we talked about slope as the change in y divided by the change in x from point A to point B. See if you can find the change in y from point A to B. I'll be back to check in a few minutes."

The teacher's feedback provided a scaffold for the student—"Remember we talked about" and gave a hint for how to move forward.[22]

This kind of constructive feedback contrasts with evaluative feedback, which tells the students whether they are right or wrong and, if they are wrong, provides the solution. With evaluative feedback, especially when it conveys a negative evaluation, there is a danger that students will see themselves as recipients of information rather than active participants in their own learning. When students are provided with good-quality informational feedback, they are more likely to use it to confirm their self-efficacy, and as a source for future learning.[23]

Good-quality feedback from teachers can be a significant factor in students' regulatory processes in several ways. First, it can lead students to a deeper understanding of the learning goals and success—an understanding they need for their self-assessment. Second, when students are prompted by feedback to take action, it can help them develop a repertoire of learning strategies by figuring out what works best in which situations. And third, when students can consider feedback and decide if and how to use it, the authority is transferred from the teacher to the student, increasing the students' potential for self-regulatory capacities. The ways in which teachers' feedback can support self-regulation are well summed up by high school students who explained that "suggestions are still making us think," and pointed out that suggestions could be "added" into students' own ideas to "give a different way" and allow them to "decide for ourselves how."[24]

External feedback from peers can also assist self-regulation. While peer feedback may not be as substantive as teachers' feedback, it has value for both the giver and the receiver in building self-regulation capabilities. Indeed, in the view of a high school student, peer feedback has a special quality: "In this class, we get peer advice. Whereas in other classes, we get teacher advice. And so, peers and teachers think different ways, because not only are we a different generation, but we both have different experiences in school and life."

When peers provide feedback, they internalize the learning goals and success criteria in the context of someone else's work, "which is less emotionally charged than one's own work."[25] Thus, they are deepening their understanding of the intended learning—an understanding that will help their own self-assessment efforts. Providing feedback about their peers' work can help students develop the skills to make judgments against goals and success criteria. These skills are transferred when students self-assess and make decisions about moving their own learning forward.[26] When peers provide suggestions for improvement, they offer another means for thinking about learning strategies that might be appropriate in a specific context. And when students receive feedback from a peer, they can find it to be more accessible because of the peer language used and the proximity both students have to the current learning and to their experiences.

Here a second-grader comments on peer feedback: "The kids can give you feedback, not only the teachers just because you can learn more stuff, and what you can also do is you can apply it to your work and it can help you. The teachers aren't the only ones who can do that [provide feedback]; the kids can actually really help each other."

And an eleventh-grade student reflects on the value of three sources of feedback, including that from peers: "We also get teacher conference time . . . and I particularly like that. Because then you get another secondary opinion behind peers, but it's very useful, because you get to have the three very different stages. You get the self, you get the peers, and then you get the teacher."

Just as self-assessment skills need to be taught, so too do the skills of peer feedback. Teacher modeling of quality feedback to their classmates will exert a powerful influence on the students' own feedback skills. These skills can also be taught through examining with students some instances of feedback and discussing what makes them effective or not. Learning how to provide feedback cannot be left to chance. Nor can it be learned quickly: the development of feedback skills will need to be sustained and nurtured throughout students' entire school experience.

To help the reader better understand the various components of self-regulation, the next section offers several cases of self-regulation, observed and heard in students across different subject areas, at different grade levels, and in different learning settings.

Examples of Self-Regulation

Self-regulation may be readily observable or audible, or both, to those around the learner. For example, a student may exhibit help-seeking behavior by physically approaching a teacher with a piece of work such as a writing assignment and asking for the teacher's reaction to a choice of words or a particularly tricky sentence formulation. In another example, an English learner may search an online dictionary for the English equivalent of the Spanish word *seguridad* (security) for a social studies essay, visibly demonstrating a tried-and-true strategy for language and concept learning. But in many, if not most instances, the self-regulation of learners may go completely undetected in the classroom and requires time and a careful ear or eye to attend to self-regulation well.[27] Throughout this book, we present different example cases to illustrate a student's development in the sophistication of language and the sophistication of self-regulation across the grades.

Internal Speech

In the first example, we use a mock-up of a middle school student's use of internal speech for self-regulatory purposes as she actively makes sense of a text she is reading (figure 2.2).[28] This example provides insights to her self-regulation.

Notice these self-regulatory behaviors:

* How the student self-monitors while she reads silently
* How she uses several self-regulation skills to comprehend what she is reading

In the third line of the text, as she monitors her reading comprehension, the student identifies some unfamiliar terminology (*L1* and *libration point*) and decides she needs to read further in the text to see if she can make sense of the terms. When she finds another unfamiliar term (*trajectories*), she tries out two strategies: first, breaking the word into component words, which she quickly dismisses as not viable, and second, determining that she needs to look the word up. Encountering again the term she was initially unsure about (*libration points*), she evaluates her own understanding of the term, making a connection to something that she is already familiar with (driving downhill). As she reads on, she comes across another term she does not understand (*solar wind*). She adopts the strategy of reading on to see if the term is explained. In the event that she does not find an explanation, she already has two other strategies in mind: looking up the word or asking the teacher. She registers her lack of understanding about *the sun-earth libration point* and employs a strategy she is familiar with, rereading, to figure out what it means. Finally, to assist her own comprehension, she consciously connects what she is reading about force with her own experience of seeing an activity that used the force of magnets.

FIGURE 2.2 A student's internal speech during reading

Libration point. I wonder what that is? Better read on to find out. [self-regulation: self-monitoring]

Okay, now I get it. It's like driving downhill; it takes less fuel! [self-regulation: evaluation]

Solar wind? What's that? I'll read ahead to see if that term is explained. If it isn't, I'll have to look it up or ask my teacher. [self-regulation: planning, help seeking, and feedback]

I'm getting a picture in my head of an activity I've seen. A paperclip was attached to a string and suspended in air because of the force of the magnet. [self-regulation: self-monitoring]

Following launch aboard a Boeing Delta II rocket, the Genesis spacecraft will travel to a point in the solar system called L1. It's a libration point, and these are special points, located throughout the universe, that can be used for low fuel trajectories (paths that require less-than-normal fuel). These points are called libration points. Librate is a verb that means to swing slightly in opposite directions, like the needle on a bathroom scale when it is coming to rest. An object librates because it is being affected by two opposing forces. Libration points in space are places between the two orbiting objects where the gravitational force exerted by the objects on each other is balanced. The Genesis spacecraft will remain at one of these libration points and collect solar wind for two years.

As the earth journeys around the sun, the location of the sun-earth libration point stays constant with respect to these two solar system objects, but moves from the perspective of a fictional observer hovering over the Milky Way galaxy in a spaceship. An object, natural or man-made, which is at one of the libration points will remain stationary, as observed from Earth, unless acted upon by some additional force. A satellite can also be made to orbit one of these points. After its nearly three-year orbit, the spacecraft will return to Earth.

L1? Did I get that right? Better read to make sense. [self-regulation: self-monitoring]

Trajectories. Since I can't break it down into smaller words, I'd better look it up. [self-regulation: flexible use of strategies, help seeking, and feedback]

Huh? I didn't get that. I'd better reread it. [self-regulation: self-monitoring]

Source: Mary Lee Barton and Deborah L. Jordan, Teaching Reading in Science (Aurora, CO: Mid-continent Research for Education and Learning, 2001), 108.

This student is clearly employing reading strategies that she has been taught. What makes this case an example of self-regulation is that she is actively monitoring her comprehension while she is reading, making determinations about when the text is confusing or when terms are unfamiliar and selecting from a repertoire of learning strategies she has built up over time to meet her goal. Her internal speech has served her regulatory processes as she articulates to herself the problems she encounters and their solutions.

Think-Aloud Tasks

In the following example, students who were part of a university-based initiative on assessment development were presented with a selection of tasks explicitly designed to elicit their thinking. These tasks were used to test the developers' understanding of students' cognitive processes that would otherwise have to be studied only indirectly or possibly go wholly undetected by both researchers and teachers.[29] In this study, the researchers conducted semistructured interviews (also called cognitive labs) to gather information about how well the new tasks measured fourth- through sixth-grade students' understanding of the academic use of English.[30] Students were audiorecorded as they completed several tasks designed to measure the language of mathematics, science, and social studies. This stage of assessment development provided the test developers with valuable information about students' interactions with tasks so that the tasks could be further modified or, if necessary, eliminated. The data could also be readily reexamined to reveal self-regulation processes as students worked to complete the tasks.

Students were asked to read the tasks aloud and to think aloud—a self-revelation technique in which the students verbalized their thoughts and reactions to the tasks.[31] The study aim was to capture the students' stream of consciousness while they were attending to the text. Such self-revelations uncovered the dynamics of comprehension difficulties.[32] The students were also asked to highlight difficult or unfamiliar words or phrases in the tasks. Students were then debriefed about their experiences using *retrospective introspection*. This technique requires the students to reflect back on their thoughts, beliefs, and emotions during the assessment situation to make these reflections explicit so that others can better understand their responses to the tasks. Specifically, students were asked to comment on which tasks were the easiest and which were the hardest. The following task and student response during the cognitive lab is taken from the mathematics portion of the prototype assessment.

Carlotta bought 9 packages of lemonade for $1.10 each and 2 packages of cups for $1.09 each. She sold 23 cups of lemonade every hour for 4 hours at $0.40 per cup. How much more money did Carlotta earn than she spent on supplies?

[The students were told not to answer the mathematics question but rather to respond to the following prompt designed to elicited knowledge of the language of mathematics.]

What is the word problem asking about?
(a) How much Carlotta spent on supplies
(b) How many packages of lemonade she sold
(c) How much profit Carlotta made [correct answer]
(d) How much lemonade costs.

The following sixth-grade student reveals several aspects of her self-regulation processes during the retrospective introspection portion of the verbal protocol: "I really didn't exactly understand [self-regulation: *self-monitoring*], so I went back up to the passage and read the question that they asked [self-regulation: *flexible use of strategies*]. So then I noticed that profit is basically the same thing [as] earned . . . of how much she's earned [self-regulation: *self-monitoring*]. So it means how much profit . . . so profit means the same thing."

First, the student flags her understanding as largely flawed, suggesting she has been monitoring her comprehension of the task. But she has a strategy to address this situation by rereading the question. She then overtly acknowledges *noticing* the similarities between two words (one used in the task and one used in the accompanying question on language), again displaying the self-monitoring of her learning as it occurs. In these ways, the student is self-regulating—monitoring her vocabulary knowledge and reading comprehension, and then taking action.

Fifth-Grade Writing Class

Notice two aspects of self-regulation in the following example:

- How the student is self-monitoring her writing process
- How she requests feedback from her teacher when she encounters a potential problem she is unsure how to solve

This case comes from Ms. Luna's fifth-grade writing class, where the students are learning about argument structures. So far, they have learned about arguments and counterarguments and are now using these structures in their own writing. Ms. Luna's instruction occurs within the predictable routine of a writer's-workshop setting. Each session of the workshop begins with a mini-lesson, in this instance, argument structure, which is followed by a period in which the students engage in independent writing, using what they learn in the mini-lesson to further their work. Ally is working on her draft when Ms. Luna comes to sit beside her and engages in the following conversation:

Ms. Luna: Okay, Ally, what are you working on?

Ally: I'm working on my final draft, and wanted to make it kind of a better sentence. [self-regulation: *planning*] And I wanted your feedback. [self-regulation: *self-monitoring; help seeking & feedback*]

Ms. Luna: Okay. Do we have our success criteria here, our checklist?

Ally: Yes.

Ms. Luna: What are you looking at right now? What are you focusing on? Are you focusing on punctuation? Are you focusing on grammar?

Ally: I'm working on this one. [self-regulation: *attention control*]

Ms. Luna: Oh, clarity. So you're asking yourself if this is going to make sense to somebody who had no idea. So what do you think so far?

Ally: I don't know if I should, because I started with two questions and then I ended with a period. And then I started another question. [self-regulation: *self-monitoring*]

Ms. Luna: I see. So let's read it and see how that makes sense.

From Ally's opening statement, it is apparent that she is soliciting assistance in her writing; she is asking her teacher for feedback. She is focused on the success criterion of clarity, which Ms. Luna elaborates as "You're asking yourself if this is going to make sense to somebody who has no idea," acknowledging Ally's self-monitoring process, possibly through internal speech, and the girl's agentive role in her learning. Ms. Luna invites Ally to expand on her request for feedback ("What do you think so far?"), and in response, Ally identifies the cause of her concern. Demonstrating her self-regulatory processes, she articulates her problem as "starting with two questions."

At this point, the exchange then moves into coregulation, with the teacher providing feedback to support Ally's revisions. We will see how such coregulation works and will provide other examples of coregulation in chapter 4. But from the perspective of self-regulation, after Ms. Luna provided feedback to Ally through coregulation, the teacher returned back to Ally the management of learning, with this statement: "So go ahead and think about how you can do that." In light of the feedback she has received, Ally is invited to consider how to move her own learning forward and take her own next steps. In the context of formative assessment, self-regulation has occurred through Ally's self-monitoring, her recognition of a potential problem, her request for her teacher's feedback, and her decision about how to use the feedback she has received. In this case, improving her writing skills is the target of Ally's learning. Her self-regulation aids in her efforts to take the reader's perspective into account. Moreover, the very interaction with Ms. Luna requires Ally to participate in a series of conversational exchanges. She must follow her teacher's requests for further elaboration and be able to clearly explain her thinking to Ms. Luna about her attempts to combine the two questions.

Whole-Class Review of Solving Fractions

Notice this feature of self-regulation in the following example:

♦ How Alex exhibits self-regulation in the context of the class discussion

In a previous lesson, fourth-grader Alan and his classmates had been asked to share a candy bar in equal portions with members of their small groups.[33] There are two groups of eight students and one group of nine students. They have been tasked with finding how much more candy each person in one of the smaller groups received than a person in the larger group. There is disagreement during the whole-class review of their previous work. Carolyn Maher is serving as their mathematics instructor for this unit. The students are asked to create a number line of zero to one on the overhead projector and to place, in order of size, $\frac{1}{2}$, $\frac{1}{3}$, $\frac{1}{4}$, $\frac{1}{5}$, and $\frac{1}{10}$.

> **Dr. Maher:** Oh. Jilly thinks one-tenth should go in the middle [of the line].
>
> **Students:** (mumble no)
>
> **Dr. Maher:** You disagree. Joe?
>
> **Joe:** I think it should go more toward zero.
>
> **Students:** (mumble yeah)
>
> **Dr. Maher:** More toward zero? Dylan? Alan?
>
> **Alan:** I think that the one-tenth should be moved over just a tiny bit. [self-regulation: *self-monitoring*]
>
> **Dr. Maher:** It's getting hard to do this, isn't it?
>
> **Alan:** Yeah. Up there, you have a whole, you are dividing it into tenths, and you have a half mark. So you have to use this as a guideline. [self-regulation: *flexible use of strategies*] You'd have five-tenths on one side and five-tenths on the other side. Now, up there, if you took that little space between the zero and the one-fifth, and you use that five times, it wouldn't reach the halfway mark. [self-regulation: *self-evaluation*]

Alan's response to Dr. Maher gives us a glimpse into this student's self-regulation behaviors because he has to give aloud a rationale for his positioning of the $\frac{1}{10}$ mark on the number line. His thinking shows that he is engaging with what previous students have said and is monitoring how his own response fits in with what Jilly and Joe have said. Alan would modify their answers just a little. The most explicit feature of his self-regulation during this episode is perhaps when he says, "You have to use this as a guideline," referring to using the halfway mark on the number line as a strategy to know where to place the different-sized fractions. Alan also shows how he considers the responses given so far and evaluates the merits of what is currently on the number line relative to their ability to reach the halfway mark (he points out that the size of the existing intervals for $\frac{1}{5}$ on the number line will unlikely be sufficient to reach the mark).

While this exchange is brief, the task and ensuing classroom discussion have elicited from Alan some comments that show several of his self-regulatory processes. This example also shows that student self-regulation can be occur throughout the school day, in many classroom configurations (whole group, small group, pairs), and not just in one-on-one consultation with the teacher or through special elicitation techniques in controlled conditions that we saw in an earlier example. Other likely opportunities to observe students' self-regulation are when they are getting started on a new task or when they get stuck on a task and solicit teacher or peer feedback.

Language Practices Supporting Self-Regulation

As Natalie Bohlmann, Michelle Maier, and Natalia Palacios explain in their study of language learners in preschool, "language takes on a primary role in regulating children's behavior."[34] Whether a student is interacting with teachers and peers in the classroom, reading about new learning strategies and practices, or receiving oral and written feedback from a teacher, language is clearly an important conduit for a student's self-regulation. The self-regulatory process starts as early as the preschool years and involves (1) students becoming increasingly able to use language to support their own metacognitive thinking—that is, to combine their critical thinking skills and language competencies; and (2) students learning to comprehend the intentional communication of others.[35] These interactions with others (teachers, peers) will initially mediate students' learning experiences and their self-regulatory development in classroom settings. For example, teachers might expressly call on students to help them break into the classroom discussion; partners in small groups ask each other questions or direct each other's attention to stay on task to get their joint assignment completed.

One well-known classroom practice is *accountable talk*.[36] Teachers use this practice to scaffold students' adoption of an academic-language register to improve content learning. Accountable talk promotes listening actively to the discussions of others to build on each other's ideas, focusing on the accuracy of what is being said. The practice requires precision of language use and attending to the creation of logical and coherent arguments. Close attention to this kind of language use in the classroom by teachers can support the development of self-regulatory skills and can hone students' abilities to control their attention, inhibit distracting or irrelevant information, plan their responses, and self-monitor the accuracy of their contributions to class discussions.

In terms of linguistic support of the development of metacognition, students often verbalize their actions and inner thoughts (i.e., private speech) as they work through challenging tasks and consider new ideas and concepts.[37] For example, in the preceding example of a student revealing her self-regulation through her internal thoughts during reading, the same student may, under different circumstances, verbalize other self-regulation dimensions wherever she finds a text particularly taxing. This kind of verbal self-expression is critical for the types of problem solving, planning, and contemplating strategies that are part of self-regulation. Students must also learn to comprehend the directions and requests of their teachers and others who would initially help the students with the actions that constitute their learning experiences. This help is external and largely verbal. For example, a teacher might orally request a student to underline all the unfamiliar words in a reading passage so that the student can return to the words and use the cumulative context of the reading passage to intelligently guess their meaning. Over time, students come to internalize these verbalized actions and procedures and use them autonomously in their own planning and monitoring of the successful implementation of tasks.[38]

Language also plays a role in flexible learning strategies, a key self-regulation dimension. When actively listening to others' discussions to build on each other's ideas, students need attention control. Focusing on the accuracy of their own responses and the precision of their language choices, students will need to self-monitor. Language skills also come to the fore when students are creating logical and coherent arguments, which are vital to many aspects of self-regulation, such as attention control, planning, and self-monitoring. In summary, language skills can help sharpen students' abilities to control attention, inhibit distracting or irrelevant information, plan out their responses, and self-monitor the accuracy of their contributions to class discussions.

Teachers can deliberately include this wide range of language use in the classroom, knowing they not only can facilitate students' oral language and literacy skills but also can support the development of the students' self-regulatory skills. For example, teachers can encourage more in-class conversation or have students generate their own questions on a newly encountered topic. (This gives a teacher insight into student questions from the perspectives of both the content knowledge questions can reveal and their level of language sophistication through a question's sentence structure.) Teachers can also build in discussion activities to their lessons and use impromptu turn-and-talk or pair-share techniques during their lessons. Such techniques are brief episodes of conversation on a particular topic designated by the teacher and are intended to help students rehearse their thinking or exchange ideas before participating in a large group discussion.

Self-Regulation Practices Supporting Language Development

The previous section examined the role of language in the development of self-regulation. On the other hand, of course, self-regulation has important consequences for language learning; most of the preceding examples show how self-regulation can promote language learning. For instance, one study reports that "better-regulated children elicit more complex language from others in their social environment. That is, adults may perceive well-regulated children as more attentive and more advanced in their language skills."[39] When teachers promote self-regulation in classrooms, their students' reading and writing abilities improve. Researchers found, for example, that among second-grade writers, self-regulated strategy development improved the students' strategic behaviors, knowledge, and motivation, particularly when the children were paired with a supportive peer who was a more competent writer.[40]

Motivation, which, as we have seen above, plays a strong role in self-regulation, also spurs language development, particularly in the acquisition of an additional language. Student motivation is important to make plans, to use strategies flexibly for language learning, and to monitor their own learning. Differences in motivation can account for great individual variation in how quickly students acquire an additional language.[41]

Self-regulation has also been tied to specific aspects of language learning for English learners. Various aspects of self-regulation have been used as strategies that can assist English learners with their acquisition of an additional language both in the classroom and during assessment. For example, English learners acquired science vocabulary better when they were expressly taught to set their own vocabulary learning goals and to self-monitor their progress.[42] Measures of students' abilities to commit to goals, to self-monitor, and to control their own concentration, among other skills, can help teachers identify the self-regulatory traits needed for the students' successes in English vocabulary development.[43]

Communities of Practice

In chapter 1, we introduced the notion of communities of practice as a setting in which all students participate with the express goal of continuously advancing each other's learning. Self-regulation is primarily an internal activity, but when a classroom is conceived of as a community of practice, there are significant advantages for self-regulation. For instance, students' feelings of self-efficacy are more likely to be enhanced when they believe that their teacher and peers see them as competent learners. Supporting self-efficacy does not mean telling students how great they are, but rather showing them that their learning is taken seriously and supported by each member of the community, no matter what their current level of learning is. As discussed in this chapter, feedback, both internal and external, is a key element of self-regulation. In a community of practice, feedback is enabled by supportive relationships, as opposed to evaluative ones, and by a genuine desire on the part of all to advance learning and to regard feedback as worthwhile. As we have seen, self-regulation requires language, and vice versa. In communities of practice, language propels learning through the internal speech of individuals and through collaboration. When students collaborate with one another, they must regulate the ways they explain what they know and be conscious of their peers' knowledge and how well their peers understand their explanations.

In the next chapter, to explore the notion of socially shared regulation, we focus on the ways in which peers interact and collaborate.

Questions and Suggestions for Teachers

1. How do you determine the levels of self-efficacy beliefs and motivation among your students? What levels of self-efficacy and motivation are evident among your students?

2. How often do you ask your students to think aloud as they are reading? What can such a practice reveal to you about their knowledge of unfamiliar words and their reading comprehension? What dimensions of self-regulation do they already deploy?
3. Next time your students ask for feedback on their writing, ask them what they notice most needs their attention. Assist them in choosing a goal to improve their writing, and help them plan strategies to achieve that goal. Ask them to think about how they will know when they have met the goal.
4. How do you promote self-regulation among your students? After reading this chapter, did you discover specific actions you could take to enhance self-regulation?
5. To what extent do you think your classroom operates as a community of practice? How could you enhance your classroom as a community of practice?

Use the student observation protocol that follows as a resource to help you observe your students' self-regulatory processes and to determine where your students need more support.

Student Observation Protocol: Self-Regulatory Learning Processes

Use this protocol to observe the self-regulatory learning processes being used by each student in your class. It's best to observe students regularly and in a range of classroom settings and activities. Doing so will allow you to cover the entire class in a time frame that works for you.

- Note the name of the student you are observing, the date, and the setting in which you are observing them. You will want to observe each student multiple times in different circumstances.
- For each self-regulatory process you see the student using, make a star by the relevant box in the accompanying diagram, and jot down any descriptive notes that may be helpful.
- Note what language the student has (or has yet to acquire) for each of the self-regulatory processes he or she is using.

- Note if the student uses a combination of strategies (e.g., a student may seek feedback for his or her planning). You can draw a connecting line between the strategies on the diagram, and note how the strategies were combined.

After completing the protocol for all the students in your class, you can use the results to see which self-regulatory processes may need to be developed more for individuals, groups, or the class as a whole. You can also see if certain situations elicit different regulatory processes among students, and consider ways to support students' language development to promote self-regulated learning.

Student name: _____

Date: _____

Context of observation (content area, working with partner or small group, etc.): _____
_____
_____

Goal setting

Planning

Self-evaluation

Self-motivation

Help-seeking and feedback

Attention control

Self-monitoring

Flexible use of strategies

CHAPTER THREE

Socially Shared Regulation

Learning Through Collaboration

*The beauty in being able to collaborate with peers is
that they have experienced the same struggles as you
[have experienced] in completing the task at hand, which
enhances their ability to give you honest feedback.*

—ELEVENTH-GRADE STUDENT

The eleventh-grader's comment sets the stage for this chapter. The students value the opportunity to collaborate because of their shared experiences. Their feedback to one another is more meaningful, and they accept joint responsibility for their learning.[1] *Honest* feedback means that they are taking seriously their responsibility to support each other's learning. This chapter develops the idea of collaborative work and the stance of joint responsibility for learning as socially shared regulation.[2]

In chapter 2, we focused on self-regulated learning, which entails students setting and monitoring goals, engaging in self-appraisal and self-management so that they adapt learning strategies when necessary in pursuit of those goals. We also underscored the influence of students' academic self-efficacy beliefs and related motivational beliefs on self-regulation.

This chapter builds on these ideas in the light of socially shared regulation, one of the two forms of social regulation (the other form, coregulation, will be discussed in the next chapter). Students do not stop self-regulating as they engage in learning with others. However, when students work with peers, they need to be more than just skilled in regulating their own learning; they must also know how to plan, monitor, wield effective learning strategies, and obtain feedback in paired or group learning situations for the good of the collective. They must combine their self-regulating processes with those of their peers and cooperate, negotiate, and manage their joint behaviors.[3] Students rely on a constellation of social cognitive abilities to learn collaboratively in group settings. These abilities are emphasized in college- and career-ready standards.

In the real-life dialogue examples in this chapter, we have added several other strategies to the list of self-regulatory strategies and related behaviors introduced in chapter 1 (table 1.1). We added these elements to fully characterize the conversations of students with teachers and between students as they work together in pairs or larger groups. First, we modified self-motivation, self-monitoring, and self-evaluation to characterize socially shared strategies. *Shared motivation* applies to learners' behaviors and dispositions that motivate their peers to engage in continued dialogue and problem solving. *Shared monitoring* refers to the behaviors and dispositions that help track the pair's or group's problem-solving progress. Finally, *shared evaluation* means the behaviors and dispositions that assess the successes of the shared problem solving, with an eye to adjustments to similar future tasks.

The examples in this chapter also show that to engage in socially shared regulation, students used additional strategies specific to working with others:

- *Nomination*: During their interactions, students offer to their peers ideas or actions.
- *Summarizing*: A pair or larger group of participants (including a teacher) summarizes the discussion so far to generate agreement or sustain momentum in the interaction.
- *Negotiation or management*: Students (or teachers) make suggestions or take control of the pair's or group's problem solving and other interactions.

In this chapter, we also address the role that language plays in socially shared regulation. If students are to productively collaborate in school, they must know how to participate in collaborative interactions as competent speakers and listeners.[4] As with self-regulation, language is the medium by which teachers can support students' acquisition of socially shared regulation. And the regulation, in turn, enables students to participate in collaborative classroom discourse.

In this chapter, we'll describe socially shared regulation as the egalitarian, interdependent, or collectively shared regulatory processes used for attaining collaborative goals. We will discuss how participation in a pair or a larger group can promote language learning. We'll also show how interactions with others can, in turn, support the development of socially shared regulation, and we'll provide classroom examples of each. Another topic we'll address is how formative assessment by teachers and students can capitalize on socially shared regulation to support language learning while the students focus on content learning. Finally, we focus on examples of socially shared regulation evident with English learners and how teachers can expressly support the students' language and content learning in collaborative settings.

Broadening the Focus from Self to Others

Figure 3.1 shows where interactions around a common task or objective between students and their peers and teachers fit within the larger system of regulatory processes for learning.

As researchers working in the area of self-regulated learning began to integrate social settings into their study of self-regulation, they observed differences in self-regulated learning during paired or group situations. They found that while students still need individual self-regulation to participate in goal-oriented behaviors with others, they also need additional types of behavioral controls and dispositions to learn in social situations such as collaborative learning environments.[5]

Simple instances of controlling others' behaviors are plentiful. For example, when a group goes off-track in a collaborative learning task, one of the group's members, noticing the time, urges his peers to get back to the task at hand so that they can complete their assigned collaborative work before the end of the lesson. In this way, students are collectively responsible for the management of their group's work. Or a first-grade student points out that collaborating with others helps her. She has already learned the value of collaboration and knows how collaboration works: "I like to

FIGURE 3.1   Socially shared regulation in the overall scheme of regulatory processes in learning

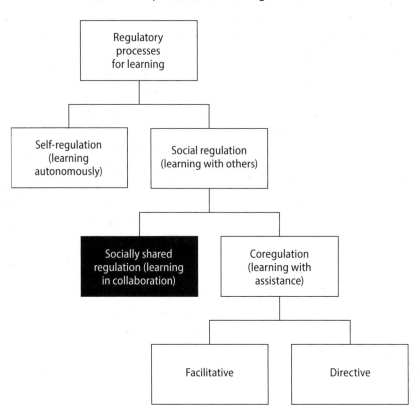

collaborate with my research buddies. Then it really helps me. That's why I like to collaborate with people. So when I'm going to research lab sometimes, we go on the iPads and search up what we need if you don't have the answer. You search it up, and then sometimes it asks us a question and we don't know it. We each take turns instead of just fighting over it."

The use of the term *socially shared regulation* can be traced back to 2003 and a study of paired interactions during a mathematics lesson with fourth-grade students.[6] Socially shared regulatory learning refers to the processes that students need to collaborate (i.e., negotiate and coordinate their behaviors toward meeting a common goal or outcome). Specifically, socially shared regulation is "interdependent or collectively shared regulatory processes, beliefs and knowledge orchestrated in the service of a co-constructed or shared outcome/product."[7] At the very least, students need to coordinate or synchronize their own self-regulation behaviors with those of others when collaborating in the classroom.[8]

This eleventh-grade student, in conversation with two classmates, sums up the benefits of socially shared regulation to their learning:

> Okay, and when we did actually talk about that [diction] because a lot of people did end up having diction as one of the ideas they wanted to use for a whole paragraph. So it didn't just help ourselves, it helped everyone, because we all realized, "Oh, this is something we all need to do." Rather than just being, "Oh, this is something I need to change." We realized that everyone had the same issue, so it was helpful that we all got to not just self-reflect, but everyone got to get input on that.

An Example of Additional Strategies in Action

To illustrate the idea of socially shared regulation and the additional regulatory processes such regulation entails, we present an exchange among three other students from the same high school English language arts class that we encountered in chapter 1.

Notice two aspects of the students' behavior in this example:

- How the students use a range of regulatory processes
- How they listen to, and build on, each other's contributions to come up with a goal for moving forward

Sophie, Gael, and Julie are considering the written feedback provided by peers on their first draft of the graphic novel that they have jointly developed. Their teacher, Mr. Allen, has asked them to think about the feedback and respond to his question "What do you have to do to take the story to the next level?" In their exchanges, the students jointly plan how to respond to the feedback. Notice how they are implementing the characteristics of self-regulatory processes discussed in chapter 2. However, because they are working collectively, they maintain an additional focus on constructing and maintaining agreement about the next steps.

Sophie: What they thought we needed more of was [inaudible] transitions . . . to make the story more fluid. [*goal setting*]

Gael: I don't think we should, like, take away too much from the mystery of the character. So then I think we should just add some subtle details. [*goal setting*]

Sophie: So I guess that would be adding more frames into the story. [*nomination; planning*]

(Mr. Allen joins the group)

Mr. Allen: So how is it going so far?

Julie: Well, we needed more transitions to improve the clarity of our meaning. So we were going to add in more details between our scenes. [*summarizing; shared monitoring*]

Gael: Another thing we want to do is maybe add a quote at the end. [*nomination; planning*]

Sophie: So just to tie in the entire message really well . . . just add the ending quote. [*summarizing*]

At the beginning of this exchange, Sophie suggests a goal for the group in light of the feedback, which recommended more transitions. Gael offers a second (and possibly alternative) goal for the group: the addition of subtle details. Sophie builds on Gael's proposal by suggesting that the next step "would be adding more frames into the story." Gael offers another suggestion, "another thing we want to do is maybe add a quote at the end," and this suggestion is reinforced by Sophie when she summarizes the plan and its purpose: "so just to tie in the entire message really well . . . just add the ending quote."

Socially shared regulation also embraces the broad areas of competence for deeper learning that we introduced in chapter 1: cognitive, intrapersonal, and interpersonal. Each one includes a cluster of competencies (see figure 1.3), some of which are evident in the high school example. For example, in goal setting and planning to respond to feedback, the students are using cognitive processes and strategies. They are also showing intellectual openness and an ability to evaluate their work. Finally, they are collaborating with each other to develop their next step.

In the following sections, we elaborate on the additional demands placed on students for successful participation in socially shared, regulated learning. Students will need to know how to learn collaboratively and develop the requisite social cognition to understand a partner's or the group members' perspectives.

Collaboration in the Classroom

In her recent review, *Thinking Together and Alone*, Deanna Kuhn outlines the developmental progression of collaborative skills in school-age students.[9] Collaboration, she says, has its origins in young children's development of joint attention skills. As these skills develop, they share an object with another person and eventually realize that others can have different perspectives on the world. (We'll discuss this realization, or social cognition, in detail in the next section.) Children learn to coordinate these different perspectives over time and have different levels of collaborative abilities. Kuhn concludes that "it is not enough simply to put individuals in a context that allows for collaboration and expect them to engage in it effectively. Intellectual collaboration is a skill, learned through engagement and practice and much trial and error."[10] Without sufficient skill development, children may fail to benefit from collaboration.[11]

Pragmatic skills (described below) and collaborative language skills clearly help with successful collaboration. Students must be able to make clear assertions if they are to successfully suggest, or nominate, an action for their collaborators to consider. Students must also be able to summarize succinctly other students' verbal and nonverbal contributions to the group's work. To do so, by the norms of most classrooms, they will need to use polite language involving question formulations that often function as requests or even commands (e.g., "Do you want to go first with the cubes?" and "Can you put the red cube on the left side?") and sentence structures that include the modal verbs (such as *could*, *may*, *should*, and *might*) needed to negotiate planning with peers (e.g., "We could put the red cubes together first").[12]

Pragmatics, the socially appropriate use of language, is a domain of language that students bring to bear on their interactions with others. Students need to know how to take turns, provide wait time for partner responses, and listen actively to their collaborators' ideas and build on them. One study found that popular children were more able to take turns and were more strategic in verbal and nonverbal communication than were unpopular children. For example, popular children could make elaborate arguments and monitor group members' facial expressions. Consequently, they were more likely to be better collaborators.[13]

Social Cognition

Not only does socially shared regulation require the development of collaborative behaviors and related language and pragmatic skills, but it also requires social cognition. Various aspects of social cognition include theory of mind (perspective taking), empathy, self-awareness, and an understanding that behavior has consequences (cause-and-effect relationships). Theory of mind involves the understanding that others may have mental states (e.g., desires, beliefs, and knowledge) that differ from one's own.[14] Although theory of mind is largely developed during early childhood, individual differences in this type of social cognition place students on a continuum of social understanding during the school-age years. This continuum is reflected in children's varying social interaction skills.[15]

Without sociocognitive competencies, students will be at a disadvantage in understanding the mental states and, relatedly, the causes of, or motivations for, the actions of others. Such understanding is a vital aspect of successful collaboration. In the exchanges among the high school students presented earlier, they could not have built an agreement had they not been aware of the potential differences in individual perspectives among the group. Their social skills in navigating the perspectives enabled them to make the final plan about their next steps and how to accomplish them. Sociocognitive competencies can be developed in young students as well. In chapter 4, you will see an extended example of these competencies in an interaction between two second-grade boys, where one student is at pains to find out if his feedback made sense to his partner and was useful.

Language Practices That Support Socially Shared Regulation

Besides the language and pragmatic skills contributing to collaboration outlined above, students also need explanatory language skills. Using effective explanatory language, students can give clear explanations of regulatory processes such as their goals, plans, and learning strategies to their group partners to justify their selection or explicate these further. These explanations require students to have control of precise vocabulary and complex syntactic structures and to coherently use temporal and logical connecting words (*first, finally, as a result of, because,* etc.) in discussions.[16]

Students must also use language to manage or coordinate the ongoing meaning making of the group. They may manage a discussion with techniques as overt as signaling their lack of comprehension to other speakers because of performance factors: perhaps the others are speaking too quietly, speaking incoherently, or speaking over one another. Alternatively, managing discussions during collaborative tasks may take subtler forms. Perhaps some students do not respond when they are expected to contribute. Or they may appear to steer the conversation in another direction because they disagree with another student's goals and plans, or they might make substantive contributions to the group's work.

By using language skillfully, students can contribute to the articulation of the plans and actions of groups or partners to achieve shared learning goals. They can be metalinguistically aware, meaning they consciously reflect on their own and other's language choices and meaning.[17] And they can be sensitive to the needs of their audiences in terms of supplying the requisite information or level of detail both during face-to-face communication and in their writing.[18]

Socially Shared Regulation Practices That Support Language Development

Socially shared regulation is, in turn, important for language learning. Students need such competence to participate in student-to-student dialogue, joint assignments, and collaborative projects as outlined above. They need socially shared regulation in all the tasks that require students to use language to get things done together. Interactions requiring socially shared regulation provide the context for the use of complex linguistic constructions and a range of discourse types (e.g., argumentation, counterargument, recounting, and explanation) that are emphasized in the college- and career-ready standards.

The next case highlights the complex interplay of these different discourse types during classroom discussions. We return to Ms. Garcia's combined first- and second-grade mathematics lesson we encountered in chapter 1.

Notice the following aspects of socially shared regulation in this example:

- How the teacher steers the dialogue so that the students come to an understanding of even numbers
- The maturity of the students' interactional skills as they challenge and justify arguments

During a discussion about grouping eight beads of two colors to make patterns for a necklace, the conversation took a different turn when one student proposed the idea of eight as an "equal" number because it could be divided evenly into two groups of four. Another student challenged that idea, arguing that all numbers are equal, since they can always be divided in two: "I think every number is an even number, because if you take a five, for example, you can split it into two and two, but then you take the extra one and you split it in half." This proposition led to a discussion of fractions, and then whole numbers, which helped lead students to define an even number:

Diego: When you split a one into halves, it's called zero point five, zero point five. So if you put one half in one box, and the other half in another box, so it would be two point five in total both. [*nominating*]

Ms. Garcia: So I would be taking that one, and splitting that one in half, that what you're saying is that I would then put a zero point five, zero point five, which in other words, represents half. [*summarizing*]

Diego: Two point five and two point five in total. [*summarizing*]

Ms. Garcia: So one would be two point five, and here I would have two point five. So were we able to split five equally? [*summarizing*]

Nora: I don't agree. Because I feel like this is not exactly, how do I say this, it is a number, but in some senses it's not. Because like, ah, how do I say this? [*help seeking & feedback*]

Jeremy: Points are basically . . . they're basically numbers, but they're numbers within other numbers. [*help seeking & feedback*]

Ms. Garcia: So a fraction of a number?

Jeremy: Yes. A fraction. [*summarizing*]

Ms. Garcia: Now I heard someone use the word "whole." Was that you, Jaime?

Jaime: Yeah.

Ms. Garcia: So tell me a little bit more. Because they're talking about a fraction of a number. And if we were able to take that five and split that five equally . . . two point five and two point five, that's equally, but . . . [*goal setting*]

Jaime: A whole number's just a regular number. Not two point three or anything. [*nominating*]

Ms. Garcia: So two point five would not be a whole number?

Jaime: No.

Ms. Garcia: But it would be equal amounts. Now we said that eight was an equal number, but seven was not, right? But now there's another word, and Jaime mentioned the word "whole," saying, yes, it's equal amounts, but it's not a whole number. So Nora, I think, yes, eight can be broken up into equal parts. Can seven? Well, five was right. But Jaime, you said, or Jaime, Marcos, you said that eight is an even number. What's even? Go ahead. [*goal setting*]

Marcos: It's a number made up of two of the same whole numbers. [*nominating*]

Ms. Garcia: Okay. So if I have eight and we're saying eight . . . would eight be even?

Marcos: Yes, because four and four are the same number and they're both whole numbers. [*summarizing*]

Ms. Garcia: So you're saying that even numbers, when we partition them or break them apart, if I can do it evenly, equally, like four and four, then that would be an even number. [*summarizing*]

Marcos: But they have to be whole numbers. [*nominating*]

Ms. Garcia: They have to be whole numbers. "Even" has to be whole numbers, and it has to be . . . We have to be able to divide it equally into a certain number of groups. [*summarizing*]

Ms. Garcia: So in order to be even, they have to be whole numbers? Now, Marcos—I mean Diego—you disagree with Marcos? [*flexible use of strategies*]

Diego: Yeah, I disagree with Marcos, because you can just split it six and if you would have to split it into two boxes, six and six and you have one more and you split the one into, so it would be zero point five again. But two zero point five, so the answer would be six point five each. [*flexible use of strategies*]

Marcos: Yeah, but it's not a whole number. [*nominating*]

Ms. Garcia: So, there's a big difference, right? I'm noticing that there's friends who are agreeing [and] others who disagree. But I really do think . . . Do you think we're talking about two different things here? In terms of even, odd numbers, and equal amounts? [*summarizing*]

Jeremy: I think they can come together. [*monitoring and goal setting*]

Ms. Garcia: You think they can come together? [*goal setting*]

Jeremy: 'Cause maybe the person who meant it equal didn't just mean equal. Maybe he meant whole two. [*nominating*]

Ms. Garcia: I don't know. What were you thinking? You mentioned the word "equal," right, Nora? [*summarizing*]

Nora: Well, I meant equal and odd, but I don't think this is exactly . . . Two point five is not a whole number. I was talking about equal. What I mean is about, it has to be, like, a whole number, not exactly like a two point five thing. [*summarizing*].

Ms. Garcia was a participant in the socially shared regulation, guiding the discussion so that the students could explore the idea of even numbers. Throughout the discussion, the students challenged each other's thinking, presented their arguments and justifications, and ultimately reached a conclusion about what an even number is. Contrast the learning that the students engaged in here with what would have occurred if Ms. Garcia had foreclosed their discussion and given them a definition of an even number. In this collaborative situation, the dialogue provided a powerful opportunity for learning about the topic under discussion. It also enabled the more knowledgeable students to extend their learning and allowed the less skilled to learn from their peers.

In the area of writing instruction, interventions have included reciprocal peer-revision strategies to improve students' writing.[19] Linda Allal describes students working in pairs as a form of coregulation.[20] However, her studies include students in collaborative interactions that require them to use socially shared regulation as well. Other studies that indirectly speak to the impact of socially shared regulation on language learning include Shufeng Ma and colleagues' research with fifth-grade students.[21] The quality of peer interactions affects the acquisition of new words, including academic vocabulary needed in the students' science curriculum, for example. This finding was attributed to the opportunities to acquire and use new words during the discussions that occur in collaborative work. Furthermore, studies have also reported positive associations between theory of mind (as argued above, a prerequisite of socially shared regulation of learning) and the vocabulary abilities of school-age children.[22]

Example of Language and Sociocognitive Demands

The following example illustrates socially shared regulation and the specific language and sociocognitive demands entailed in an exchange from an algebra lesson on exploring linear functions.[23]

Notice two aspects of the interactions:

◆ How each student contributes to the management of the group
◆ How the students engage in self-regulation during their collaboration

Six seventh-grade students have been introduced to the Guess My Rule activity by Mr. Peters. The boys are sitting in a semicircle on chairs in front of the classroom whiteboard. Projected on the board is a square (representing the independent variable) separated from a triangle (representing the dependent variable) by a vertical line. These two shapes represent the unknown rules that will transform the first number into the second. Mr. Peters gives the boys the first pair of numbers (five and thirteen) and then asks the students to extract the rule that could account for the number five being transformed into thirteen and to also predict what would happen to another number (three) that the boys then choose. Andy has just begun to articulate what the meaning of the square and triangle might have for coming up with a solution. Levi wants to quieten the other boys down so they can all hear Andy repeat and elaborate on his contribution.

> **Levi:** Let Andy talk. [*negotiation; management*]
>
> **Mr. Peters:** Okay, Andy, go ahead.
>
> **Andy:** All right, so, like, the square could be the number you're putting in, and it can say, like, it can go to, like, the factory, or something like that. And it come out the number in the triangle, triangle number. Square number and triangle number. [*nomination; planning; flexible use of strategy*]
>
> **Mr. Peters:** Okay, so did you hear what Andy said?
>
> **Levi:** Yup, he's mad smart. [*shared motivation*]
>
> **Garret:** No, he talks too fast. [*help seeking & feedback; negotiation; management*]
>
> **Mr. Peters:** Jonas, could you tell us what Andy said?
>
> **Jonas:** Umm, I didn't hear him. [*negotiation; management*]
>
> **Garret:** He talks too fast. [*help seeking & feedback; negotiation; management*]
>
> **Jonas:** Can you repeat that again, please? Can you repeat that? [*negotiation; management*]
>
> **Andy:** The square could be like a type of number, and then when it goes into, say, like a factory or something like that. It would

come out the triangle type of number. [*nomination; planning; flexible use of strategy*]

Garret: So, square is a number and triangle is a factor? Is that what you trying to say? [*summarizing; negotiation; shared monitoring*]

Levi: Look, look. It's like the square is, like, the bigger kind of shape, and then the, like, triangle goes into the square to make . . . [*attention control*]

Jonas: It keep on multiplying by four.

This example highlights group negotiation or management and related language in socially shared regulation at the same time that we see evidence of students still drawing on self-regulation aspects, such as monitoring and attention control. Specifically, Levi, Garret, and Jonas all contribute attempts at management of the group, focusing on the auditory quality of Andy's speech. They are clearly having trouble hearing him.

Andy is the only student in this exchange to nominate a new idea and a plan to solve the problem when he attempts to use the analogy of a factory (possibly the notion of a production line) as a learning strategy for the generation of the input and output of numbers.

Unfortunately, the boys do not take up this analogy to help their problem solving. Jonas explicitly asks Andy to repeat the factory analogy, and Andy slows his speech down (being responsive to several requests by this point) and explains the meaning of each shape within the frame of his factory analogy. Garret tries to succinctly summarize and then to monitor the group's comprehension of Andy's explanation by asking explicitly "So, square is a number and triangle is a factor? Is that what you trying to say?"

There could be some continued confusion due to mishearing Andy say "factor" for "factory." Andy himself may have been influenced by the mathematical term *factor* when he thought up the factory analogy. With Andy slowly laying out the meaning of the shapes, Jonas eventually sees a pattern in the numbers and attempts to extract (albeit still incorrectly at this stage) a rule for the square and triangle placeholders that would account for transforming five into thirteen ("multiply by four").

Formative Assessment Through Social Channels

As discussed in chapter 1, formative assessment informs learning, rather than measures it or sums it up. Teachers conducting formative assessment plan to intentionally obtain evidence of student learning against established criteria during the course of a lesson and involve students in the assessment process through self-assessment and peer feedback. As we have seen in the examples so far in this chapter, socially shared regulation of learning occurs through interaction. These interactive settings can provide teachers with evidence not only about students' thinking with respect to the goals of learning, but also about language learning and, indeed, the students' capacities to engage in collaboration.

For effective formative assessment, collaborative settings need to engage students in the kind of dialogue that both promotes and reveals learning. To this end, Micheline Chi and Muhsin Menekse have proposed a hypothesis for considering dialogue between pairs: the constructive-active-passive hypothesis. We believe that this hypothesis also applies to larger group interactions. The components of the hypothesis are as follows:

- *Passive*: The partner listens and utters agreement (e.g., "Okay," "Right").
- *Active:* The partner listens and describes what has been stated or repeats what was stated by the other partner.
- *Constructive:* One partner elaborates on what he or she said previously or what his or her partner said.[24]

Working in pairs, the partners may take on various combinations of roles. For example, one partner may be passive while the other is active, both partners may be active, or one partner may be constructive while the other is passive. In collaborative learning situations, learning is promoted when both partners adopt a constructive stance in the dialogue.[25] When students are engaged in socially shared regulatory processes, they will learn better when each person participates in constructive dialogue. In constructive dialogue, the participants elaborate on what they or another person has just said, as Andy and Jonas did in the previous example. Through such elaboration, students' thinking is more clearly revealed to a teacher for the purposes of formative assessment.

To illustrate formative assessment in the context of socially shared regulation, we return to Mr. Allen's high school classroom where the groups of three students are writing their graphic novels.

Notice some features of the discussion:

- How the teacher uses interactions as a formative assessment opportunity

◆ How the students build on each other's ideas throughout their conversation

At the beginning of the lesson, Mr. Allen asks the groups to review together an exemplary graphic text to "identify the essential elements of a graphic text and essential elements of an allegory." The students will develop criteria from the model text for writing their own graphic novel. After Adrian, Liza, and Kim, another group of students in this classroom, review their text, the following conversation ensues.

Adrian: The words are supported by the pictures, and vice versa.	
Liza: Especially in terms of characterization. So once we are drawing it, it's going to be very important to portray the character through the visuals.	*Constructive:* elaborates on what Adrian said
Kim: You won't need to describe as much as you did in a normal text. Instead, it's very sparse in terms of words, but the pictures take care of the rest of the explanation.	*Constructive:* elaborates on what Adrian said
(Teacher joins the group)	
Mr. Allen: So have you guys come up with any essential elements for allegories or graphic texts from looking at this exemplar?	Assessment question
Kim: It's just using the deeper meaning to get the explicit out of it.	
Mr. Allen: What do you mean by explicit?	Assessment question
Liza: In this graphic text, we really noticed that the use of mice as characters really furthered the message.	*Constructive:* elaborates on what Kim said
Mr. Allen: What are some of the deeper levels of meaning that you have gleaned from the text?	Assessment question
Liza: Well, it's talking about the philosophy of the way you live your life, and that's the implicit meaning in that text.	*Constructive:* elaborates on the group discussion

Kim: That's something we'll have to focus on when we are doing our own graphic novel.

Constructive: elaborates on what Liza says

Mr. Allen: I just want to make sure that you guys are clear about the explicit and the implicit meaning.

Assessment prompt

Adrian: Explicit is the surface level of the story. For instance, the tortoise and the hare. If one was to look at it with the explicit meaning in mind, then it would be about a tortoise and a hare that had a race. But the implicit meaning is always keeping . . . uh . . . putting effort in, or others who are more hungry than you in terms of ambition will overtake you.

Constructive: elaborates on the group discussion

(Liza and Kim nod)

As you can see from the exchange above, the students' individual comments mainly fall into the *constructive* category. Also note how the teacher uses the group's interaction as an occasion for formative assessment; he asks several questions to probe the students' understanding of explicit and implicit meaning. His final prompt provokes a response intended to reassure him that the students do understand the difference between implicit and explicit meanings, which will be essential knowledge for writing an allegory. The *constructive* dialogue revealed the students' thinking and academic-language usage provided evidence of their ability to collaborate around a topic.

The students' language usage itself also shows how several of their contributions are linguistically tied to one another and how the students build on each other's ideas. For example, after Adrian starts out by saying, "Words are supported by the pictures, and vice versa," Liza elaborates on this further by saying "especially" and then giving the example of characterization as an instance of Adrian's claim. In places, they paraphrase or use synonyms for each other's word usage (e.g., "pictures" used by Adrian becomes "visuals" for Liza). Such paraphrasing shows how group discussions can be a rich source of language exposure when different people express ideas in several ways.

Communities of Practice

The kind of discussion by Adrian, Liza, and Kim in this exchange and in the other examples in the chapter so far does not necessarily occur naturally among K–12 students. Instead it has to be explicitly taught and nurtured by teachers in a community of practice. A primary concern in a community of practice for socially shared regulation is establishing norms of respect and trust between teacher and students and among students. Without feelings of trust among students, students are not willing to take the risks necessary for learning.[26] Students must feel able to contribute their ideas, reveal their thinking, and respond to the ideas of others without fear of ridicule or sanctions. Beyond establishing norms, Sarah Michaels and Catherine O'Connor propose four foundational goals for productive discussions.[27]

Goal 1: Helping Individual Students Share Their Own Thoughts

If a student is going to participate in a discussion, he or she has to share those thoughts and responses out loud, in a way that is at least partly understandable to others. Establishing classroom norms of respect and careful listening and letting students practice speaking aloud can help them share their own thoughts. In Ms. Garcia's classroom discussion, the classroom norms permit students to express their own ideas and to build on the ideas of others, even respectfully disagreeing with their peers, as in this instance: "Yeah, I disagree with Marcos because you can just split it six and if you would have to split it into two boxes, six and six and you have one more and you split the one into, so it would be 0.5 again. But two 0.5, so the answer would be 6.5 each."

Goal 2: Helping Students Orient to and Listen Carefully to One Another

If a student is just waiting to speak, and is not *listening* to others and *trying to understand them*, he or she cannot contribute to a real discussion. The ultimate goal involves the sharing of ideas and reasoning, not simply a series of students giving their own unconnected thoughts, one by one. An example of this kind orientation and listening occurs in the preceding exchange between high schoolers Sophie and Gael, who were working on their graphic novel. Gael says, "I don't think we should, like, take away too much from the mystery of the character. So then I think we should just add some subtle details," and Sophie builds on that idea when she responds, "So I guess that would be adding more frames into the story."

Goal 3: Helping Students Deepen Their Reasoning

Most students are not skilled at pushing to deepen their reasoning. A key role of a teacher is to continuously and skillfully press the students for reasoning and evidence. Asking questions such as "Can you say more?," "Can you give us an example?," "Why do you think that?," "What is your evidence?," and "What led you to that conclusion?" can help students extend their thinking and explain their reasoning. We see Ms. Garcia consistently taking on the role of pressing students throughout the entire student discussion.

Goal 4: Helping Students Engage with Others' Reasoning

Real discussion to support learning occurs when students take up the ideas and reasoning of other students and respond to them, as in a dialogue characterized by constructive exchanges. In the classroom examples we have seen so far, constructive exchanges are a predominant feature.

When teachers attend to these goals, they provide a useful guide to develop students' own discussion skills. These goals are also foundational to teacher-guided discussions, which, in turn, provide powerful models for students' own interactions.

Example of English Learners in a Social Learning Setting

While much of the existing research has focused on classroom discourse as observable (audible) instantiations of socially shared regulated learning, no studies, to our knowledge, have explicitly examined what language and literacy characteristics students need to participate in effective socially shared regulated learning. Likewise, we know of no studies that examine whether socially shared, regulated learning (beyond the collaborative setting in which this learning most often occurs) itself leads to more effective language and literacy learning. Yet students who are often put on the periphery of classroom collaborations, such as English learners, may find themselves on the outside of discussions because they lack the language or pragmatic skills and experience to be involved in this social type of learning.[28]

More than any other students, English learners would benefit from effective collaborative learning situations (resulting from control of socially shared, regulated learning behaviors) because these are potential sites of rich language input. For example, Shufeng Ma and colleagues' findings suggest that "high quality discussion may lead to better lexical representations . . . [G]ood lexical representation contains sufficient knowledge of orthographic, phonological, and semantic properties of words for people to retrieve the words rapidly and flexibly . . . Students in collaborative groups, especially, may develop dense and integrated networks through constantly presenting claims and responding to classmates' claims and challenges during collaborative discussions."[29]

The following example looks at English learners in dialogue with one another. The young students in the first exchange are preschoolers working in pairs on an arts/science inquiry task.

Notice two aspects of the children's dialogue in this example:

♦ How students use their first language to engage in regulatory processes
♦ The range of regulatory processes they engage in

First, preschoolers Betty and Paola are mixing liquid paint using a variety of colors from small paint droppers. They are standing over their large sheets of paper at their desks in their preschool classroom. They are both dominant in Spanish, and their preschool teacher uses both Spanish and English with her students.

> **Betty:** ¿Puedo hacerlo con mi dedo también? ¿No? ¿Lo puedo hacer con mi dedo? [Could I do it with my finger too? No? Could I do it with my finger?] (is referring to mixing paint) [*help seeking & feedback*]
>
> **Paola:** ¿Verdad que está suave? ¿Está muy suave verdad? [It is smooth, right? It is really smooth, right?] [*help seeking & feedback*]
>
> **Betty:** Siiiiii. [Yes]. [*shared motivation; shared evaluation*]
>
> **Paola:** Este si está suave. Porque cuando haces con tu mano así, si está suave. [This one is smooth. Because when you do it with your hand like this, it is smooth]. [*flexible use of strategy; shared evaluation*]
>
> **Betty:** Si verdad. Le voy a poner más. [Yes, that is right. I am going to put more on.] [*shared evaluation; planning*]
>
> **Paola:** Yo también. [Me too.] [*planning*]
>
> **Betty:** Agarra ese. [Grab that one.] (points to an additional paint dropper) [*nomination; flexible use of strategy*]

This exchange shows socially shared regulation taking place in the students' first language. The use of their first language should be encouraged in such situations. A student's dominant language may be best for developing regulatory processes, especially early on in language development because it allows the student the best opportunity to express himself or herself fully. Betty and Paola's dialogue covers a range of regulatory processes that begin hesitantly with the self-regulatory process of help seeking and feedback (e.g., "Could I do it with my finger too? No?"). But the conversation becomes more synchronized and far more resolute as both girls plan to use their fingers to mix the different colors of paint on the paper ("Le voy a poner más [I am going to put more on]" and "Yo también [me too]"). While some of their language consists of simple sentences and is quite repetitive, when Betty elicits feedback on her idea to use her finger, her language is notably more complex (including the use of the modal verb *puedo* [could]). Similarly, when Paola explains the consequences of her learning strategy to Betty (using her finger to paint) and evaluates the result (smooth paint), she produced a complex sentence structure to convey the causal connections ("porque cuando [because when]").

A final example is from another pair, this time an exchange between Angelika and Elena during a fourth-grade mathematics lesson. Incidentally, this example shows the dominance of English by this later grade; there is just a smattering of Spanish, even though these students are also English learners.

Notice two aspects of socially shared regulation in this example:

- The kinds of questions they ask and how they support socially shared regulation
- How the students jointly manage their interaction

The two girls are working as a pair to predict whether a tack shaken in a cup will land flat side up or down. The object is to learn about the principles of probability.[30] One student is tasked with writing down their prediction, and the other shakes the cup and reveals which side the tack lands on.

Angelika: Okay, the prediction for the next one. Hmm. [*negotiation*; *management*]

Elena: Call it again now. [*nomination*]

Angelika: Up. Yeah! [*shared motivation*]

Elena: Well, but why do you think that they all land up, up? [*help seeking & feedback*]

Angelika: Porque [because] most of the time it's, it's landing up, up, porque [because] not all porque mira . . . [because look]. Like right now (pauses), up (pauses). It doesn't land like inside

all the time . . . It always lands like . . . most of the time end up.
[*attention control*; *summarizing*]
Elena: Okay, so, like, put "up"? [*help seeking & feedback*]
Angelika: Up.
Elena: And up it is! [*shared motivation*]
Angelika: Up it is! [*shared motivation*]

The short exchange reveals a wide range of socially shared regulation processes at play in just this simple prediction task. The girls are managing one another's behaviors, nominating actions, eliciting feedback, controlling attention, motiving each other, and providing a summary explanation. In terms of feedback more specifically, this consisted of their open-ended questions that are both syntactically complex and may encourage deeper discussion (e.g., "Well, but why do you think that they all land up, up?"). There was also an informally worded request to simply affirm what should be written on their joint worksheet (e.g., "Okay, so, like, put "up"?). The open-ended question by Elena gave Angelika a real opportunity to take stock of her own learning before she responded with the explanation for Elena. Angelika's explanation, however, is hesitant (many uses of "like"), contains several retraces or false starts, lacks coherence, and does not actually answer Elena's question about why tacks land facing upward.

Strategies for English Learners

What can be done to assist students who are on the periphery of social interaction in the classroom?

Here we pay special attention to the situations of English learners to describe how they can become full and productive participants in classrooms while they are also acquiring English as an additional language. These strategies go beyond the four foundational goals for productive discussions described above and explicitly focus on the language that students need to engage in socially shared regulation. Although we recommend the following strategies for English learners who may still be on the periphery of much classroom participation, these techniques for inclusion may also work equally well with native-English-speaking but still-reticent students who find it hard to engage in collaborative work with classmates.

- Give students the language and pragmatic behaviors needed to collaborate in pairs or small groups (e.g., how to verbally signal their monitoring of progress, how to communicate feedback to and elicit feedback from others).

- Make student pairings thoughtfully: pair up English learners with peers who are sympathetic conversationalists and who can provide effective feedback.
- Give English learners time to reflect on their participation.
- Share ideas of how English learners can learn.
- Model giving feedback to real errors and, if necessary, create instances of fictitious language and content errors to provide further opportunities to model feedback.

This list of strategies, though not exhaustive, provides a starting point for teachers to develop their own approach. The goal is to ensure that all students have the chance to reap the benefits of socially shared regulation for both learning and developing the language competencies that we have outlined in this chapter.

In the next chapter, we turn to another form of regulatory process: coregulation. We examine how coregulation can be a temporary support for the self-regulation and socially shared regulation that we have discussed in previous chapters.

Questions and Suggestions for Teachers

1. How do you promote socially shared regulation among your students? After reading this chapter, have you come up with some actions you could take to enhance your students' socially shared regulation?

2. When your students are working in groups, take some time to listen to their dialogue. Note how much the dialogue falls into active, passive, or constructive categories. If students' dialogue is not predominantly in the constructive category, think about how you could help your students build on each other's ideas.

3. Consider the four foundational goals for productive discussion, and reflect on your own practice. Are there any goals that you think you need to strengthen? If so, how might you do that?

4. In your class, are there students who could benefit from the strategies outlined at the end of the chapter for use with English learners, or are there students who are otherwise reticent to participate in collaborative work?

In the accompanying protocol, we provide a resource for capturing your students' use of the socially shared regulation-specific processes introduced in this chapter.

Student Observation Protocol: Socially Shared Regulatory Learning Processes

Use this protocol to observe the socially shared regulatory learning processed used by students working in pairs or larger groups in your class. It's best to observe students regularly and in a range of classroom settings and activities. Doing so will allow you to cover the entire class in a time frame that works for you.

- Note the names of the students in the group you are observing, the date, and the setting in which you are observing them. You will want to observe each student multiple times under different circumstances.

- For each socially shared regulatory strategy you see this group of students using, make a star by each box, and jot down any descriptive notes that may be helpful.
- Note what language students have (or have yet to acquire) for each of the socially shared regulatory processes.

After conducting multiple observations with the protocol, you can use the results to see which socially shared regulatory processes students may need to develop. You can also see if certain situations elicit different regulatory processes among students, and consider ways to support students' language development to promote socially shared regulatory learning processes.

Student names: _____

Date: _____

Context of observation (content area, working with partner or small group, etc.): _____

_____

_____

CHAPTER FOUR

Coregulation

Assistance for Learning

The kids can give you feedback, not only the teachers,
just because you can learn more stuff. And what you can
also do is you can apply it to your work and it can help
you. The teachers aren't the only ones who can do that;
the kids can actually really help other people.

—SECOND-GRADE STUDENT

As this quote from a second-grade student indicates, support for learning does not only come from teachers. This young student is clear that peers can be a resource for each other's learning. In this chapter, we examine learning support for self-regulatory processes from both teacher and peers in the form of coregulation, the second form of social regulation. Coregulation most commonly refers to regulation of a student's learning by a teacher or a more regulated peer.[1] It serves as a temporary support for acquiring self-regulatory and socially shared regulatory processes.[2]

As discussed in chapter 1, coregulation (sometimes referred to as *other regulation*) is rooted in the concept of socially mediated learning and the idea that humans learn through culturally based communication that builds and shares knowledge.[3] Coregulation is grounded in intersubjectivity and scaffolding. Intersubjectivity involves participants in a shared perceptual focus and shared activity around a common task.[4] For example, in previous chapters, we have seen students engaged in common tasks, such as the high school students revising their graphic novel draft (chapters 1 and 3), Ally and Ms. Luna focused on Ally's writing for the purposes of feedback (chapter 2), and seventh-grade students engaged in an activity to explore linear functions (chapter 3). Scaffolding refers to the assistance that is provided to learners to solve a problem, carry out a task, or achieve a goal that would be beyond their unassisted efforts. We have seen several instances of scaffolding throughout the preceding chapters, including the scaffolding role that Ms. Garcia adopts in her interactions with Aidan (chapter 1) and in the group discussion on even numbers (chapter 3), Lucy's guidance of her peer Sarah (chapter 1), and Mr. Allen's discussion with students about implicit and explicit meaning (chapter 3).

In coregulation, thinking is distributed between the individual doing the scaffolding and the individual who is appropriating the knowledge and skills as a result.[5] The coregulation taking place progressively transfers to self-regulation so that the self-regulatory processes that learners initially cannot undertake on their own gradually become part of their independent achievement.[6] In the case of Ally and Ms. Luna from chapter 3, for example, we can imagine that when Ally encounters the issue of putting two questions back-to-back in a future writing task, her own self-regulatory processes will take over and she will no longer require the assistance of her teacher.

In figure 4.1, we highlight which processes this chapter will focus on within our larger framework of regulatory processes for learning.

Coregulation, the second of the two types of social regulation characterized in the research literature as part of the regulatory system, can be further characterized by whether the coregulation offered by a teacher or peer leads to the successful transfer of regulation of the learning process to the student who is the target of their assistance.[7] As figure 4.1 indicates, coregulation can be *facilitative* or *directive*. In facilitative coregulation, supportive, collaborative learning groups and effective teacher scaffolding transfer the regulation of learning to the individual. *Directive* coregulation, on the other hand, may help a student complete a specific task but does not help the student regulate his or her own learning. For example, a teacher or peer might impose his or her own planning and goals on the learning situation or might take over the choice and implementation of learning strate-

FIGURE 4.1

Overview of regulatory processes for learning: where coregulation fits

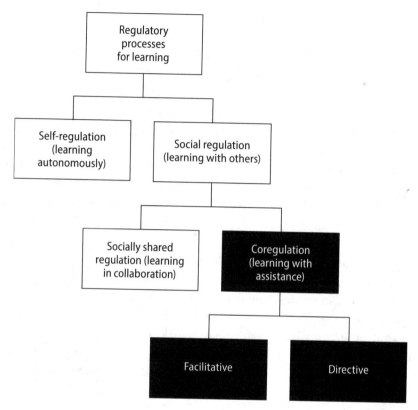

gies. Such directive behavior could include reading a passage for the novice reader or giving the answer to a mathematics word problem. Whatever its form, directive coregulation can lead to less positive outcomes for the learner in terms of motivation and transference to self-regulatory processes.

Throughout the chapter, we will address how, as Allyson Hadwin and her colleagues put it, the interactions between teachers and students and among peers "temporarily mediate regulatory work (strategies, monitoring, evaluation, goal setting, and motivation)."[8] In other words, we'll look at the collaborative interactions that help students acquire the self-regulatory processes described earlier.

As in prior chapters, we illustrate coregulation with classroom case studies and show the synergistic relationship between language and co-regulation. Given that most coregulation of students' learning experiences will take place through conversation with students or written feedback on student work products, the ability to comprehend oral and written language for coregulatory purposes are imperative. For example, students need to understand the teacher's prompts, probes, and elicitation of reflection. They also need to produce descriptive and explanatory language and make statements that convey reflection and understanding.

Coregulation, as a key mechanism for acquiring self-regulatory and socially shared regulatory skills, will of course be implicated in students' own language learning. Coregulation of learning by teachers, such as scaffolding a student's attempts to self-monitor her word choice in a research report (e.g., "Does this word make sense here? Have you checked if there is another word like this that you can use instead of repeating this one throughout your writing?") and teacher's provision of other contextual supports (e.g., posted steps and strategies; cards with transition words for structuring reports; posters of hints for getting unstuck when writing stories) can assist a student's language and literacy development. Eventually, these kinds of questions and suggestions can be internalized by the student who is being assisted so that the student will become self-sufficient in making learning strategy choices and can independently self-monitor his or her own steps to completing tasks.

Let us move now to a deeper examination of coregulated learning.

Coregulated Learning

Through coregulation, teachers may most effectively and directly support students' development of self-regulatory learning.[9] With scaffolding and other contextual supports, for example, routines and guided participation, students can internalize learning processes and make them their own.[10] For instance, when teachers provide a student with a breakdown of component steps to more effectively accomplish a new task, or when they give a student feedback on different aspects of progress on a particular task, they are controlling the learner's experience (i.e., the flow and arrangement of new information, corrective input) in order for learning to more effectively take hold. In these situations, they are also modeling socially shared regulatory behaviors and dispositions (i.e., working collaboratively toward the shared goal of increasing the novice learner's knowledge).

This tenth-grade student describes the coregulation that occurs when teachers provide feedback on a particular task: "When we first write the essay where it's just us on our own with our own ideas, then once we turn it in it's the teacher helping us a lot more. With the feedback, which I think helps a lot, once we do the revisions I believe we get a lot more in-depth into the essay. Think about it more, and start thinking about our ideas and how to get it across better."

Receiving, Judging, and Acting on Assistance and Feedback

For successful coregulation, learners must have three attributes: (1) receptivity to suggestions and feedback on their learning behaviors; (2) an ability to judge the value of that information for their continued learning; and (3) a willingness to act on the assistance and feedback being offered by teachers and peers. Abilities in these three areas are often likely to be taken for granted by teachers and others working with students. However, if students are to be the beneficiaries of coregulation in the classroom, teachers need to know how their students are making sense of the proffered assistance and feedback and how to support these fundamental precursors to successful coregulation.

This tenth-grade student expresses well an openness to feedback and her willingness to use the feedback to become a stronger writer:

> The revision process really helps me become a stronger writer and a stronger learner. I'm not afraid to make mistakes. I know that with this feedback, I can take it, and if I don't get it right on the mark the first time, I know I do have a second chance. I really feel like that's part of life. You're not going to do everything perfect the first time. You do get second chances, and I think it really develops [you] into a stronger writer. I remember at the beginning of the year, I didn't do so well on my first writing assignment. As I applied the feedback and did revisions, I learned to create the better connections and become a better writer.

Students also need the ability to elicit effective feedback from others. Rather than patiently waiting for others to notice that they need help, self-regulated learners know when and how to get others to help them, as we outlined in chapter 2.

At a very basic level, to benefit from coregulation, students need to understand the pragmatics of coregulation—that is, the socially appropriate behaviors expected of students during interactions with their teachers and peers. These behaviors range from knowing the rules for taking turns in an academic setting, to the polite language we use in seeking and acknowledging others' input. For example, students learn to phrase requests as questions or statements, such as "Can you help me? I would love your help," rather than as commands, like "Help me!" Teachers can model these pragmatically appropriate behaviors by voicing the various polite openings and bids that students can use for eliciting feedback: "Excuse me, I would like to get your thoughts on my explanation of this math procedure. Does it make sense to you?" "Could you follow my directions?" "Is my question about penguin habitats clear to you? How can I make it more detailed?" They can also model gracious ways to receive feedback, especially when it may not always be favorable: "Thank you for your feedback, this will improve my report; I think your comments will help me revise my answers."

Such uses of language convey to students an openness and deep appreciation of others' proffered opinions and suggestions about their work. Appreciation of others' input to a task is an undervalued yet important aspect of student collaborative interaction.[11] Appreciation, a characteristic of communities of practice discussed in chapter 1, will contribute to a classroom climate in which students will feel motivated to offer suggestions to one another and safely receive critique as valuable feedback to improve their learning.

The aspects of coregulation described above are all *facilitative*, as identified in figure 4.1. They aim to support students' learning and their eventual uptake of the regulatory capabilities that other, more skilled students use during interactions. Let us consider this *facilitative* aspect of coregulation in the following example.

Example of Facilitative Coregulation

This example is a continuation of the exchange between Ms. Garcia and Aidan, whom we first encountered in chapter 1 in the combined first- and second-grade classroom. The students were working on composing and decomposing numbers to develop their understanding of place-value. Ms. Garcia engages Aidan in a formative-assessment conversation to gauge his understanding of his mathematical solution.

Notice the facilitative approaches Ms. Garcia takes:

- The various scaffolding practices that Ms. Garcia uses
- How Ms. Garcia supports Aidan's self-monitoring

Ms. Garcia: What do you know about the question? What does it seem to be asking you? [*establishing intersubjectivity; attention control*]

Aidan: Um, to add up how many baseball cards they have.

Ms. Garcia: So it seems that your answer was greater than the number you started with, right? [*attention control*]

Aidan: Yeah.

Ms. Garcia: So it seems to me that you've unpacked the problem, right? [*attention control; self-assessment*]

Aidan: Yeah.

Ms. Garcia: You're coming up with a strategy that fits well with the way the problem is structured here—right?—and you're explaining your strategy. Do you think you have met the success criteria for this lesson? Do you think you have met the goal? [*self-monitoring; self-evaluation*] Let's go back and look at it. (she reads the first part of the written goal that is displayed on the table) Today, your goal as a mathematician is what? [*attention control; intersubjectivity*]

Aidan: (continues reading) To represent your understanding of a one-step word problem.

Ms. Garcia: Do you think you represented understanding of a one-step word problem? [*self-evaluation*]

Aidan: Yeah.

Ms. Garcia: I think you did, and you even went back and you're checking your work. That's great. This is what I am going to suggest (points at Aidan's paper). You started . . . I see you have a hundred, a ten, and a one, and you are using number discs. I want you to continue, and I want you to go back and compare your answers while I work with another partner. I know you think this answer is nine hundred sixty, and I'm not saying it's wrong—you might be right. But going back and checking your work is a great strategy that mathematicians always use, so I'm glad that you're doing that now. [*nomination; flexible use of strategy; self-evaluation*]

Aidan: Okay. So this side doesn't really show my strategy. So I should check on this side. (turns over the paper) [*self-evaluation*]

Ms. Garcia: You want to check on this one? (points at the paper)
  [*intersubjectivity*]
Aidan: Yeah.
Ms. Garcia: And remember, your answer might be right. And I'm
  not saying it's wrong. It's always good to go back and check.
  [*nomination; flexible use of strategy; self-monitoring*]
Aidan: Let me see. (looks at his paper)
Ms. Garcia: So it's always going back and checking our work. [*self-
  monitoring*]
  Well, it was great hearing about your strategy today. (Aidan
  continues to look at his paper) Aidan?
Aidan: (looks up at Ms. Garcia) Okay.

Ms. Garcia first establishes their joint attention on the paper that shows
Aidan's problem-solving strategy. This paper and the mathematical strategies that Aidan has written become a common ground for a series of
questions and answers about Aidan's solution. Ms. Garcia employs several
scaffolding practices to keep Aidan "in the field" (keep his attention and
motivation on the task at hand.[12] First, she offers expressions of interest in
his work, often using the word *notice* to signal interest. Second, she acknowledges his success ("You're coming up with a strategy that fits well with the
way the problem is structured here—right?—and you're explaining your
strategy . . . I think you did, and you even went back and you're checking
your work"). In this way, she is consolidating his practice and ultimately
"making it worthwhile for the learner to take the next step," which Marja
Vauras and colleagues say is a key scaffolding strategy.[13] Third, in motivating
Aidan to develop the habit of checking results, Ms. Garcia observes, "Going back and checking your work is a great strategy that mathematicians
always use, so I'm glad that you're doing that now." With this remark, Ms.
Garcia not only gives support to Aidan's existing work, but also reinforces
his identification with mathematics and the mathematicians who practice
it by observing that "checking work" is a hallmark of "mathematicians."
Finally, she motivates him to check his work by not confirming or discon-
firming that his solution is correct. Clearly, there is coregulative support
for checking mathematical results as an aspect of self-regulation.

Ms. Garcia also displays another element of scaffolding practice: transference of responsibility.[14] This step is particularly apparent when she leaves

the outcome of his checking deliberately ambiguous, making it clear that it is Aidan's responsibility to determine whether his answer is right or wrong. What's more, Aidan immediately initiates the task he has been assigned ("Let me see") and looks at his paper.

Ms. Garcia supports Aidan's self-monitoring when she asks for his assessment of whether he has met the learning goal ("Do you think you have met the success criteria for this lesson? Do you think you have met the goal?"). Subsequently, she returns to the written goal and criteria displayed on the table, prompts Aidan by reading the beginning of the goal. After he has read the full goal, she again prompts him for his assessment of his achievement ("Do you think you represented understanding of a one-step word problem?"), continuing to place Aidan in an agentive position relative to the overall lesson goal. Assisting Aidan in this way to focus on the overall arc of the lesson will likely help his self-monitoring, which fuels self-regulation.[15]

In terms of the language needed to support this coregulation episode, Ms. Garcia put into words what she has seen Aidan do to solve the mathematics problem. She narrates what he has done, giving him on several occasions the necessary vocabulary associated with his learning (e.g., *unpacked, problem, strategy, structured*, etc.) She also asks him to closely reread the question to be sure he comprehends what the question is asking and, consequently, whether he has answered all parts and provided exactly what the question requires. Perhaps most striking in this example is the language Ms. Garcia uses to convey her suggestions for what Aidan should do next. Her requests are couched as simple statements ("I want you to continue, and I want you to go back and compare your answers . . . But going back and checking your work is a great strategy that mathematicians always use, so I'm glad that you're doing that now").

However, the pragmatics of this situation are not really about Ms. Garcia's wants and feelings. Aidan needs to infer from these statements (I want X, and I'm glad you are doing Y) that he is being requested to carry out these extra steps of comparing his answers and checking his work. To interpret these expressed feelings as anything but a request to carry out the next steps would be a violation of the pragmatics of the coregulation interaction. English learners, especially, may miss the subtleties of the real intent of statements like these; an understanding of such subtleties is part of what it means to know a language. Such linguistic nuances are deeply embedded within a culture and can mean different things in another culture. The English learner's first language may be far more direct than English, possibly making requests in an imperative form (e.g., "Continue. Go back and check your answers, please").

Using such language also adds to a climate of caring in Ms. Garcia's classroom community. She makes her wishes known, as well as her positive feeling about Aidan's use of strategies used by mathematicians. If Ms. Garcia had not previously worked to have such a positive classroom climate and a relationship of mutual caring with her students, Aidan may have cared little about what his teacher wanted or felt glad about, and so he may have had less motivation to respond to her requests (direct or otherwise). But given such an established, positive climate, with student choice and autonomy respected and expected, Aidan has a clear incentive to care about his teacher's wishes and her contentment. He is likely to respond (consciously or not) to fulfill those as he turns back to double-check his answer.

Next we'll consider at a deeper level the role that language plays in coregulation.

Language Practices That Support Coregulation

Language has a key role in coregulated learning. Language is prerequisite for clarifying student thinking and for students to communicate their thinking to others. Teachers' conversations with students and written feedback on student work draw on both the oral and the written language abilities of students. Similarly, to help students notice and reflect on new ideas and understand new content, teachers need to teach specialized receptive and expressive vocabulary, as well as a variety of discourse skills. For example, students discussing each other's descriptions of the plot of a shared novel and where to place them on a chart of progressively more elaborate and detailed plot information will need to understand the language of their teachers' and peers' justifications (e.g., "I think you are still at a level 2 because you don't tell us where the story happens"; "You didn't explain why the main character leaves town"). Students also need these same language skills to absorb suggestions or modifications for improvement (e.g., "You might try linking his first actions to his later actions"; "Describe the conditions in which he lived so it makes sense later on why he left").

Experimental studies have shown that teachers' use of certain learning-relevant language also helps students adopt learning strategies. For example, one such study of a classroom intervention with seven-year-olds involved teachers deliberately privileging memory-relevant language during their interactions with students.[16] In these interactions, the teachers used several strategies. For example, they provided and solicited metacognitively rich information (e.g., reminding children of facts, events, or procedures). They also asked metacognitive questions (e.g., "How did you know that would work?"). Another technique was "recommending that a child adopt a method or procedure for remembering or processing information," among other deliberate strategies.[17] In this study, the teachers were using these strategies to help students learn about the science of machines that move (e.g., wheels, axles, and gears). The researchers found that these kinds of strategies "could impact the encoding and retrieval of information, such as focusing attention or organizing material."[18] As a result, these students had higher levels of strategic knowledge for solving problems and used more-sophisticated memory strategies in tasks measuring their new science content knowledge than did students who were not exposed to this kind of teacher language as input. Such findings suggest how much teachers' language practices can affect students' self-regulation.

Coregulation Practices That Support Language Development

The connection between coregulation and language and literacy outcomes has received some attention in the literature. Coregulation (between peers) has been documented to have an effect on literacy development. For example, in one study of elementary students' writing skills, teachers used coregulation to foster their writing development.[19] The study, however, may more strictly be an instantiation of both coregulation by a more regulated peer and socially shared regulatory learning in moments of more egalitarian sharing of feedback between peers. In terms of how coregulation supports language learning, teachers can explicitly model regulatory strategies as the more expert partner for students to emulate during student-student and student-teacher conversation. Setting routines for different self-regulation behaviors can also support language practices needed in the classroom more generally. This support includes the creation of mnemonic strategies to determine if all steps of a task have been completed before turning in work and using the classroom environment as a supportive resource. For example, a teacher could have the students consult classroom posters reminding them of the various strategies they might choose.

The posters illustrated in figure 4.2 were made by two first- and second-grade combination classroom teachers to hang on the walls and doors of their classrooms as reminders to their students of the many strategies available to them. Notice that these environmental supports do not simply list the different steps of a task for students to follow without reflection. Rather, the posters provide students with a menu of possible strategies that use language and literacy skills to complete their work. "What Do I Do if I Think I'm Done?" assists students in becoming their own careful editor and working with a partner to do a final check of their writing. "Mathematician's Toolbox" offers the strategies of asking a friend, rereading, and explaining chosen mathematics approaches, in other words, integrating language and literacy skills within mathematics learning. These posters remind the children of all the options they have available if they want assistance—all without the teacher's needing to be directly involved. Simply put, the posters can help build autonomy in learners.

FIGURE 4.2   "What Do I Do if I Think I'm Done?" and "Mathematician's Toolbox" posters: assisting students' independent problem solving

What Do I Do if I Think I'm Done?

- Check our work for punctuation
- Check our work for capitalization
  - Beginning of a sentence
  - Proper nouns: names of people, days of the week, months, special places
- Check for spelling
  - Sight words
  - Circle other words that you're unsure of
- Meet with a partner to double-check work
  - ☐ Adjectives   ☐ Dialogue
  - ☐ Words instead   ☐ Pictures
    of "said"

Mathematician's Toolbox

- Try a different strategy
- Ask a friend
- Double-check
  - Count 2 or 3 times
- Reread the problem
- Try an easier number first
- Choose a responsible spot and focus
- Use manipulatives
- Use color
- Explain your strategy
- Start at the beginning

Source: Used by permission of first- and second-grade classroom teachers.

Formative Assessment and Coregulation

So far in this book, we have discussed formative assessment as integral to the learning process; it is the means through which teachers and students move learning forward while learning is under way. We have also discussed that a central element of formative assessment is the feedback that students receive from their teachers and peers and that is intended to assist them in taking the next steps in learning. Feedback is a critical component supporting students' self-regulation.

We can also extend the idea of feedback to include coregulation of students' learning experiences.[20] Feedback provides a temporary support for students to think about what they are doing well in terms of progress to meeting the learning goal. Through feedback, a teacher gives students suggestions or cues to help them decide how to revise their work or performance and to help with their planning and further goal setting.

If feedback is to serve as a temporary support for self-regulation, crucially it must not provide students with solutions or correct answers. Doing so deprives students of the opportunity for reflection, decision making, and goal setting, all hallmarks of self-regulated learning. Effective feedback can also engage students in thinking about learning strategies. In other words, it can bring to students' attention possible learning strategies, for example, rereading, making connections with prior learning, drawing a representation. Feedback can also mean leaving the students to decide what is the most appropriate in the circumstances. Such a focus on learning strategies can ultimately enable students to draw from their own strategy repertoire and take action based on their own self-assessment without being consistently dependent on teacher or peer feedback.

As noted, teachers are not the only source of feedback. As the second-grader at the beginning of this chapter said, "the kids can help people." That is, they can help people by providing peer feedback. When students provide each other with feedback, they are essentially engaging their peers in the forms of scaffolding that we discussed in chapter 1. Among other activities, they can engage a peer's interest in the task, maintain attention on the task, focus on the task's relevant features, and provide support for the next step in learning.[21] In peer feedback, students do not act as each other's teacher, as in the teacher-student scaffolding role. Indeed, one peer may not have more expertise than the other. For this reason, we might characterize peer feedback as a collaboration in which each student assists the other.

This reciprocal feedback takes on the character of an egalitarian cognitive partnership between peers.[22] In this partnership, students use various social and communication skills: intersubjectivity and the ability to understand a partner's point of view, communicate one's own views, listen actively, and inhibit one's own actions.[23]

Example of Coregulation in Peer Feedback

In the following case study, we illustrate how peers, even as young as second-grader, can engage in a cognitive partnership while providing peer feedback. We will see how such coregulation provides temporary support for self-regulation.

Notice two features of the peer feedback in this example:

- The importance of success criteria for peer feedback
- How the students use a simple, but effective structure to provide peer feedback

Ms. Davies's second-grade class comprises students who are English learners, English proficient students, and students with disabilities. The students have been working on these two learning goals throughout the year:

- We are learning to read with fluency.
- We are learning to provide feedback about our peers' reading.

The success criteria for meeting these goals are posted in the front of the room. During the year, Ms. Davies has incrementally created these criteria with her students so that they understand, in detail, the performance that reading fluency entails:

- I can read smoothly, by reading words accurately and in phrases.
- I can read with expression, by expressing what the character is feeling.
- I can read with meaning, by understanding the words and paying attention to punctuation.
- I can read at just the right speed, not too fast and not too slow.
- I can give feedback that includes what has been done well and ideas about where to improve.

As the lesson begins, Ms. Davies reviews the learning goals and success criteria, inviting the students to talk about the success criteria in turn and to provide examples of each one. She then lets them know that they are going to read with a partner and provide each other with feedback. Before they begin their reading and feedback session, Ms. Davies tells them that they are going to provide *her* with feedback about *her* reading. The feedback is framed as a *star*, what she has done well, and as a *step*, what she needs to do next to improve. Ms. Davies reads aloud and first asks the students to write down her star and, after a second reading, her step. After this, she conducts a whole-class discussion where she invites her students to read out loud what they wrote about her star and her step. She reminds students of the importance of looking and listening—looking at their peers and the text and listening carefully to the read-aloud.

Now we turn to two of Ms. Davies's students, Tomás and Juan, who are providing each other with peer feedback. Because of the teacher's careful preparation, they can give specific feedback related to the performance criteria, mostly within the structure of stars and steps.

Tomás reads his passage aloud while Juan listens.

Juan: Okay, you didn't read too fast or too slow, but your step is to when you said "no," you kinda paused right there and then just kept going. [*establishing intersubjectivity; coregulation; self-monitoring*]

Tomás: Okay.

Juan: You read like the character, everywhere except for this part. I don't know if it's this part or this part. (points to a section of the text) [*attention control; self-assessment*]

Tomás: I remember not reading with expression at this part. (points to the text) [*self-monitoring*]

Juan: Yeah, it's only this part. (points to the text) So I think that's all you need to work on. [*goal setting*]

Tomás: Thank you for giving me the feedback.

Juan: Was I being honest, or do you disagree with some parts? [*self-evaluation; help seeking & feedback*]

Tomás: I agree.

Juan: With all of it?

Tomás: Yeah.

Juan: Did you understand the feedback? [*coregulation; self-assessment*]

Tomás: Yeah. Can you read it first for me so I can give you the feedback? (points to Juan's text)

(Juan reads his text aloud)

Tomás: You did read with meaning and expression, but you've read kinda fast. You've read that whole thing fast, but you've read it really good, though. [*coregulation; self-evaluation*]

Juan: So, did I have any stars? [*help seeking & feedback*]

Tomás: Yeah, your star is you were reading with expression and meaning, this whole paragraph and this one, kind of. That's my feedback for you. [*coregulation; self-monitoring*]

Juan: I understood the feedback. Thank you for the feedback.

Tomás: You're welcome. So that's all you have to work on. [*coregulation; goal setting*]

After the peer feedback session, Ms. Davies asks the students to reflect individually and, in light of the feedback they have received, to set a goal for the next time they read.

Juan first offers feedback to Tomás in relation to the success criteria for fluency. Although he does not name his first set of feedback as a star, he tells Tomás that he met one of the criteria—reading at the right speed. The step he offers Tomás is seemingly jointly negotiated. He has drawn Tomás's attention to the fact that he did not read part of the text with expression, and Tomás affirms that he did lack expression at a certain point. Tomás determines where in the text that occurred. Juan agrees and then frames his next comment as a goal: "that's [reading with expression] what you need to work on." Juan is at pains to ensure that his peer understands the feedback and agrees with it, almost as if he is encouraging Tomás to be metacognitive when he says, "Do you understand the feedback?" possibly doing this unknowingly. After Juan has provided his feedback, he also has his chance to read aloud, and Tomás reciprocates with his feedback.

During this feedback session, each peer is a temporary "expert" on the other's performance. In his temporary role as expert, each student offers support at a meta-level for the other, identifying points of success and an area to work on to improve fluency. In their interaction, both boys bring an awareness of assessment and goal setting through their feedback. This sort of coregulation allows them to potentially internalize these same processes in their own learning situations. A skilled teacher will capitalize on this potential to transfer the processes of coregulation into self-regulation. In fact, this is what Ms. Davies does when she asks students to consider the feedback they have received and to establish a personal goal for improvement.

In this interaction, we also see the emergence of sophisticated social and communication skills that, as noted earlier, are associated with an egalitarian cognitive partnership. Both students actively listen to each other reading aloud, without interruption, and communicate their own views about their peer's reading performance. Juan, in particular, wants to ensure that his peer has understood his point of view regarding his suggestions for modifications, asking Tomás if he understood the feedback Juan has given and if he agreed with it. We can easily imagine how Juan and Tomás would transfer these communicative competencies into other collaborative situations, such as joint problem solving around a specific task.

Coregulation and English Learners

Coregulation is of special importance to English learners, whose language learning can be promoted through the scaffolding of interactions between teachers and students and among students. For example, teachers can pair students with more proficient bilingual classmates and can use the student's dominant language strategically during English language instruction and other content areas whenever possible. The teacher doesn't need to speak a student's first language, but rather needs to creatively seek ways to incorporate a student's first language into their school experiences. Here are some ways all teachers, including monolingual English teachers, can coregulate the language and content learning of an English learner:

◆ Consciously place an English learner into paired or group activities with other students who share the student's first language but who are more proficient than the other student in English.

◆ Seek out other students in the school who also share a student's first language and who can become regular reading buddies in English.

◆ Enlist the assistance of adults in the school or wider community to periodically work with English learners in their first language as necessary (develop a list of such contacts and share it with other teachers).

◆ Allow students whose first language is not English to create first drafts of work in their first language. This form of instructional support does not require assistance from a speaker of the first language at all but enables students to catalogue their ideas. It gets them thinking and reasoning about different concepts and topics effectively in their strongest language before they translate this phase of their work into English.

All these scaffolding strategies can be followed up with the gradual removal of such assistance as students begin to increasingly self-regulate their language learning experiences.

Examples of Coregulation with English Learners

The following example of classroom practice from a fifth-grade writing class illustrates how the teacher coregulates the student's content understanding and her language choices.[24]

Notice the coregulation strategies Ms. Luna uses:

♦ How the teacher models the kind of thinking that self-regulated learners adopt when they are actively monitoring their writing. For example, when writing an argument, self-regulated learners may ask themselves, "What are my reasons?" or "What am I trying to say here?" or "How does this support my argument?"

Ms. Luna and Maria are having a formative-assessment conversation about Maria's writing, which attempts to persuade her reader of the virtues of recycling. In terms of formative assessment, Ms. Luna's purpose is to find out where Maria is in relation to the development of her arguments, counterarguments, and reasons. The development of these features in her writing has been the focus of learning in several class periods. During the interaction, Maria reveals a linguistic error. As you will see, Ms. Luna ultimately identifies Maria's error as one of vocabulary rather than one of misspeaking or misreading. Facing the choice of either fixing the vocabulary error or focusing on the main learning goal (the argument), Ms. Luna decides in favor of the lesson goal.

> **Ms. Luna:** Read me your argument first, just so that I understand what it is that you're . . . [*establishing intersubjectivity; attention control*]
>
> **Maria:** I think people should recycle because, like, you could help the earth get, well, clean and healthy.
>
> **Ms. Luna:** Okay. And your reasons? [*coregulation; self-monitoring*]
>
> **Maria:** To save the earth, you can provide people by getting injured when they are picking cans, bottles from the street or in the trash can.

Ms. Luna: Are you saying you could provide for people? [*coregulation; self-monitoring*] (slight nod from Maria) Read that last one again, I missed that one word.

Maria: You can provide people by not getting injured.

Ms. Luna: Let me see the word. (Maria points to the word in the "reasons" column of her notebook)

Ms. Luna: Are you trying to say . . . What are you trying to say there? [*coregulation; self-monitoring*]

Maria: People provide getting hurt.

Ms. Luna: And how does that support your argument? [*coregulation; self-monitoring*]

Maria: 'Cuz, like, 'cuz some people, they throw, um, bottles and cans on the street, so some people are like walking and they trip on the bottles on the street and they try to recycle those.

Ms. Luna: Uh-huh. And is that a good thing or a bad thing that they are picking up the bottles from the street?

Maria: Good.

At the beginning of this interaction, Ms. Luna accounts for her request, "Read me your argument," in terms of understanding what Maria's objective is. Her additional remark, "Just so I understand what it is that you're . . ." registers Maria's agency in the work and the teacher's own role as an assistant in the formation of the argument. After Maria has proposed recycling as her primary argument, Ms. Luna acknowledges this goal and then asks for Maria's reasons for her proposal. Maria's response incorporates a linguistic error; Maria uses the word *provide* instead of either *protect* or *prevent*. Ms. Luna continues the conversation, treating Maria as having articulated a satisfactory sentence in English and focusing on one of the writing goals—connecting reasons with the argument. By not distracting Maria from the goal of writing, Ms. Luna supports Maria's self-regulation as the student develops her argument. Ms. Luna can address the vocabulary error on another occasion.

In a second example of a teacher working to increase the language knowledge of English learners, the interaction helps a student develop her self-regulation and illustrates formative assessment in action. This example comes from data we collected from our recent work on the progression of students' oral and written explanations.[25] The exchange takes place in a first-grade classroom during a language arts/literacy period with English learners. While the student is required to collaborate with the teacher by taking turns during the question-and-answer participation structure, we have chosen this example primarily to illustrate how students need communicative competency to convey new content knowledge (a formative-assessment opportunity, too).

Notice an effective aspect of coregulation in this example:

• How the teacher supports the student's own self-monitoring during their interaction.

Sitting with her students on a rug in a whole group configuration, the teacher sounds out the word *hoped*:

Ms. Terry: H-O-P-E-D. Is it *hopped* or *hoped*?
Students: Hoped.
Ms. Terry: How do you know? [*coregulation; self-monitoring*]
Camille: Because it has an E-D.
Ms. Terry: But *hopped* has an E-D, too. How do we know? [*coregulation; self-monitoring*]
Camille: It has a double consonant.

In this short exchange, the teacher presses her students and asks, "How do you know?" (i.e., that the word is *hoped* and not some other pronunciation or spelling) when the class had chorally responded with the correct pronunciation of the word. By focusing her students' attention on the source of their knowledge, she is making overt the need for students to self-monitor their learning. When a student responds, "Because it has an E-D," the teacher points out that the existence of just -*ed* is not the morphological aspect of the word that indicates it is pronounced "hoped." She makes this point by stating that both *hoped* and *hopped* end in -*ed*. She continues to ask Camille what aspect of the word will tell her how it is pronounced: "How do we know?" The question signals that Ms. Terry is still looking for a different kind of evidence in the word. She is pressing Camille to continue to self-monitor her understanding of English morphology rules and pronunciation.

In this exchange, we see the teacher solicit an answer and evaluate that answer as unsatisfactory. Rather than simply signal to the student that it is incorrect, she offers the student specific feedback (a key feature of formative assessment) on why it must be incorrect (i.e., both words end in -*ed*). Then, instead of giving the correct answer to the student (which is not the purpose of formative assessment), she takes the time to stay with the same student to ask again, "How do we know?" With the range of options now narrowed down to just a few sound/symbol aspects of the word (an example of contingent pedagogy by the teacher), the student can now explain, "It has a double consonant" (we infer that she is referring to the word *hopped* and not *hoped*—she does not specify).

Gordon Wells reminds us that scaffolding of a novice learner by more knowledgeable others, be they teachers or a more regulated peer, is not the only way we can assist students in acquiring English. When second-language learners are at similar levels of language expertise, the metaphor of scaffolding the learning of another is less appropriate. Rather, Wells notes, the assistance that English learners give each other as they collaborate on an English writing task does not involve "wide discrepancy in expertise, nor is either student taking on the role of designated teacher. Most importantly, there is no deliberate intention to work toward handing over control of the task when the requisite strategies have been mastered."[26]

This distinction between coregulation among peers and coregulation with a more skilled person and a learner is important. Many teachers and students find themselves in classrooms with large numbers of English learners who are often at similar levels of English language development and are sometimes even *deliberately* placed into classrooms by comparable levels of proficiency. But all is not lost regarding the strategic use of student pairing to support language learning and, by extension, content learning. Wells considers such pairing akin to the socially shared regulation covered in chapter 3. In these situations, students at similar levels share the same task goal; the purpose is not to have one student intentionally teach the other. (The exchange between Angelika and Elena in the pin-drop experiment illustrates this point well in chapter 3.)

In most joint activities, there are multiple opportunities for learning with and from other participants. For instance, some solutions that a group creates could not have been achieved by the group members on their own. In these cases, all participants in the group progress in learning because of their joint activity.[27] As we move into the next chapter, these examples of learning created jointly with others are important reminders of the synergies that support learning through interaction.

In the final chapter, we show how self-regulation, socially shared regulation, and coregulation work in concert, and we describe what students, teachers, and school systems can do to promote these critical regulatory processes for language learning.

Questions and Suggestions for Teachers

1. When you give students a choice of learning strategies to complete a task, what precursor self-regulatory behaviors will you possibly need to support via coregulation?
2. How can you avoid being too directive when coregulating students' language and literacy learning?
3. In what facilitative ways can you give sufficient support to your beginning (intermediate, advanced) English learners so that they can pursue their content-area goals successfully?
4. When you are conducting formative-assessment conversations, do you think you are engaged in coregulation? How might you improve the way you coregulate learning in this context?
5. Which example of coregulation in the chapter do you think is the strongest? Why do you think this?

In the accompanying protocol, we provide a resource for you to examine your students and your own behaviors and dispositions during coregulation.

Student Observation Protocol: Rate Effective Use of Peer and Teacher Coregulation

Use this protocol to observe and rate students' behaviors and dispositions during the coregulation of student learning. It's best to observe students regularly and in a range of classroom settings and activities. Doing so will allow you to cover the entire class in a time frame that works for you.

- Note the names of the students you are observing, the date, and the setting in which you are observing them. You will want to observe each student multiple times under different circumstances.
- For each coregulatory strategy, rate the effectiveness of the strategy from 0 (not used) to 4 (used most productively) on the accompanying graphic. Then connect the dots to see the overall pattern (see ancillary figure with example of a completed graphic).
- Additionally, you can use the graphic to reflect on and rate your own behaviors and dispositions regularly during coregulation with different students.

After conducting multiple observations with the protocol, you can use the results to see which coregulatory processes work most effectively for different students in different situations.

Student names: _____

Date: _____

Context of observation (content area, working with partner or small group, etc.): _____

_____

_____

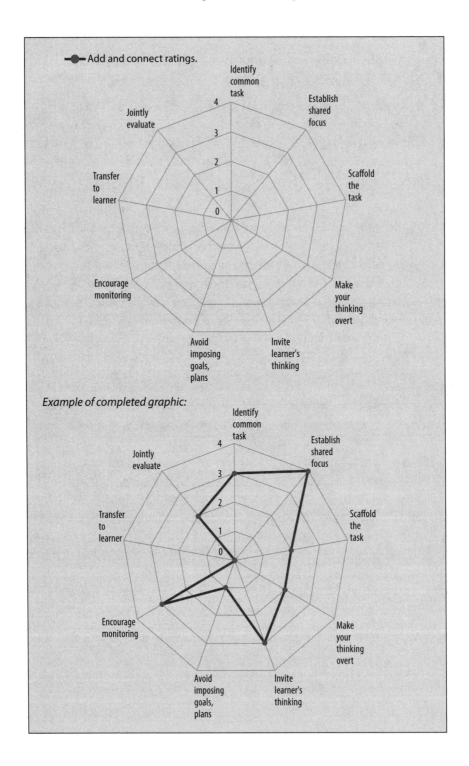

Example of completed graphic:

CHAPTER FIVE

Integration of Regulatory Processes

Transforming Classroom Practices

*My best advice is to pick one thing or two things to
start with, and give it a try, and don't worry about if it's
going succeed or fail right away because it's a learning
process for you, it's a learning process for your students.
But just know that if you keep practicing with it, you'll
find the way that works specifically for you and your
kids, and that it can be really, really successful.*

—HIGH SCHOOL TEACHER

In the prior chapters, we have focused separately on three regulatory processes. In a sense, treating the processes separately made an artificial distinction. Most research on social regulation acknowledges that self-regulation and social regulation occur simultaneously and in an interconnected way. Regulation carried out as a collaborative or group learning activity can be challenging because several self-regulatory systems must cooperate to generate and achieve shared goals.[1] Students do not stop self-regulating as they learn collaboratively or have their learning experience coregulated by a teacher or one or more peers.[2] Rather, students must combine their own planning, goal setting, self-monitoring, motivation, and so forth, and coordinate (perhaps even sometimes replace) these aspects of learning with those of others in any social regulation activity. This chapter will focus on the interconnectedness of the three regulatory processes and will illustrate their interrelation with classroom case studies as we have done throughout the book.

If the promise of regulatory processes to students' current and future learning is to be realized, educators will need to make major transformations in classrooms. The all-too-pervasive lesson design of review, demonstrate, practice fails to support the development of coregulation and socially shared regulation.[3] Not only does this common approach deprive students of the chance to develop valuable regulatory processes, but it also deprives them of powerful opportunities to learn with and from others and especially to develop language competencies.

To make the necessary transformations in practice, teachers will need deep, professional learning experiences that enable them to acquire knowledge, reflect on their own practice, and try out new ways of organizing learning in their classrooms. The high school teacher's comments at the beginning of this chapter represent a realistic, authentic strategy for effectively transforming practices to include support for regulatory processes. This teacher realizes that she needs to start with a manageable action and that she and her students have to take risks and be willing to learn from their successes and failures. She also realizes that a one-size-fits-all approach to transforming practice is not viable. Rather, she and her students have to find ways to incorporate the regulatory processes in a way that works for them.

Her comment also leads us to the *social ecology* of the classroom—the intricate system of relationships between teacher and students and between students. As discussed, these relationships, revealed by social interactions in the classroom, can either inhibit regulatory learning or, in a "learning culture," support it.[4] Students engage with teachers and each other in a classroom community that is characterized by participant-oriented learning practices. Many teachers will have to shift the social ecology of their classrooms to enable self-regulation, socially shared regulation, and coregulation.

This chapter will also address the knowledge and skills that teachers need to transform classrooms and the teacher-support systems that must be in place in schools and districts.

Let us begin by examining two cases of integrated regulatory processes.

Example of Learners Engaging in Collaborative Dialogue

The first example is from Ms. Garcia's combined first- and second-grade mathematics class. Jake (a second-grader) and Aidan (a first-grader) were working together, without teacher support, on composing and decomposing three-digit numbers to represent their problem-solving strategies. As explained in chapter 1, *composing* refers to the makeup of the number; for example, 349 is composed of three hundreds, four tens, and nine ones (300 + 40 + 9 → 349). And as discussed, *decomposing* describes the process of breaking numbers apart, as in this example: 349 → 300 + 40 + 9. Sitting side by side, the boys discuss their respective strategies.

Notice the combined regulatory processes in this example:

◆ How self-regulation, socially shared regulation, and coregulation are layered throughout the interaction
◆ How the boys use language to clearly explain their respective procedures for their mathematical solutions

Aidan: Which makes fifty here (points at representation) and here, which makes fifty. [socially shared regulation: *attention control*]

Jake: So, look, I actually used the same strategy, except you're kind of doing strategy with shape. [coregulation: *attention control*; socially shared regulation: *flexible use of learning strategies*]

Aidan: Yeah, it's like we are doing a strategy in different shapes. [socially shared regulation: *flexible use of learning strategies*]

Jake: Yeah, but what I did . . . is . . . first you decomposed them, and then you composed them.

Aidan: Yeah, because if you decompose them first and then compose them, it makes it easier. [self-regulation: *self-evaluation*]

Jake: (turns over his paper) When I did this problem, I did the same strategy except it's a little different. I composed them, still using the same thing like I was composing them, still using the same, because you can see how I first actually added them together. And then you kind of decomposed them. You first decomposed them. [coregulation: *flexible use of learning strategies*; *attention control*]

Aidan: Yeah, because you see if you compose first, there's a different number that you get to compose together so it's harder . . . But if you decompose, you get different numbers that you compose, which makes it easier. But you have to choose what you decompose carefully. Otherwise, it can make it harder. [socially shared regulation: *flexible use of a learning strategy*; *shared motivation*; self-regulation: *self-evaluation*]

Jake: Yeah, that's actually a pretty good observation. [coregulation: *shared evaluation*; *help seeking & feedback*]

As you can see from the annotations above, the two boys are clearly engaged in regulatory learning processes. The very fact that they are having this conversation in the midst of their mathematical activity is evidence of their regulatory capacities. They set and pursue their own agenda for the interaction, without any prompting from their teacher or any other external sources.

Their interaction exhibits many of the features of regulatory processes that we have described in previous chapters. First, there is intersubjectivity: the students' joint attention on each other's mathematical representation for solving the same problem, and a common ground for them to actively manage their interaction. They acknowledge that they are both using the same strategy when Aidan elaborates slightly on Jake's prior observation about "doing strategy with shape."

Second, their interaction continues through mutual scaffolding. Jake notes the strategy that Aidan used: "Yeah, but what I did . . . is . . . first you decomposed them, and then you composed them."

His comment prompts Aidan to reveal his thinking about the relative merits of the order of decomposing and composing: "Yeah, because if you decompose them first and then compose them, it makes it easier."

Responding contingently to (in tune with) Aidan, Jake elaborates on his strategy, comparing his method with Aidan's: "When I did this problem, I did the same strategy except it's a little different."

Jake reiterates his earlier observation that Aidan used decomposition first in his representation method: "I first actually added them together. And then you kind of decomposed them. You first decomposed them."

Aidan returns to the topic immediately, providing a more detailed rationale for his approach.

Third, the boys' entire interaction is goal oriented, focused on their respective approaches to developing strategies for solving the mathematical problem they have been assigned. Jake invites Aidan to discuss his thinking about the strategy he has used ("except you're kind of doing strategy with shape" and "first you decomposed them, and then you composed them"), providing opportunities for Aidan's expanded explanation, which Jake acknowledges by his final comment: "That's actually a pretty good observation." At the same time, Jake also describes his strategy by providing a contrast to Aidan's. In this way, they are constructively acquiring knowledge together, not transferring knowledge one to another. Finally, they motivate each other to consider their approaches to representing mathematical strategies, a temporary support for bringing their thinking to a conscious level for future self-regulation. Throughout this interaction, we see the integration of the three regulatory processes as Aidan and Jake engage with each other about their respective mathematical solutions.

It seems reasonable to infer, then, that Aidan and Jake, and their classmates, have learned to engage in these kinds of regulatory processes from their experiences with their teacher. The interactional models the teacher provides daily have been taken up by the students and become an integral part of the underlying fabric of classroom interaction that contributes to notion of the learning culture in which regulatory processes take place.

From a language perspective, the boys are able to coherently explain their different mathematical procedures for decomposing numbers using, for example, temporal discourse markers such as "first" and "and then." While the explanations sound rather intricate or even convoluted to the naive listener or reader, the boys maintain accurate control of the different uses of the pronoun *you* (Jake's use of "you" to refer to Aidan, and Aidan's use of "you" to mean the generic "you" or "one"). Additionally, the boys have the pragmatic skills to listen to each other's explanations, take turns, and successively add new information to contribute to joint meaning making.

In the next case, we focus on a first-grade language arts lesson with English learners. This example comes from our early work on language progressions used in the formative assessment of literacy.

Example of English Learners Arguing from Evidence in the Text

In this example, a small group of first grade students have been given the task of gathering clues from the text of a book they have just finished independently reading. Now they must collectively identify "whodunit" (i.e., determine which character in the book is the villain of the story).

Notice the integration of regulatory processes in this example:

- How the teacher uses questioning to coregulate the students' discussion and elicit the evidence she needs to assess students' understanding formatively
- How the students' language skills enable regulatory processes
- How students respond to each other's suggestions

> **Ms. Ramirez:** M. E., that's a good point. Who do you think is a suspect in this case? [coregulation: *intersubjectivity*]
>
> **M. E.:** I think Rosamond stole the picture. [self-regulation: *self-monitoring*]
>
> **Ms. Ramirez:** Why do you think that? [coregulation: *intersubjectivity*]
>
> **M. E.:** She's Annie's close friend, so maybe she really wanted to have it.
>
> **Ms. Ramirez:** What page made you think that? [coregulation: *intersubjectivity*; *nomination*; *flexible use of strategy*; *self-monitoring*]
>
> **M. E.:** (looks through the book for a minute) On page twenty-three. (all the students then turn their books to page 23)
>
> **Artemio:** I think it could have been Rosamond 'cause she was one of the only ones who saw it. But what about Annie? [self-regulation: *self-monitoring*; socially shared regulation: *nomination*]
>
> **Carlos:** Why would Annie take it? That doesn't make any sense. It was hers in the first place. [socially shared regulation: *shared evaluation*]
>
> **Artemio:** What if she lost it and forgot about it? [socially shared regulation: *nomination*]
>
> **Ms. Ramirez:** Those are all good speculations. [coregulation: *evaluation*][5]

This example shows the integration of self-regulation, socially shared regulation, and coregulation during authentic classroom collaborations—in this instance, for student collaboration. As the students are sharing ideas and working on the common task of using the text as evidence for who they think is the suspect, Ms. Ramirez supports their discussion with her questions designed to get them to first share their thinking. The children must then make ownership of their opinions evident to the others with phrasing such as "I think." Using these phrases helps the students monitor their own ideas and contributions to the discussion.

Moving the conversation along to solve the task, the students disagree with one another. They use dialogue to solve the task by overtly evaluating others' statements ("That doesn't make any sense"). But more often, they ask each other questions about the logic of the evidence they are collectively building (e.g., "But what about Annie?" and "Why would Annie take it?" and "What if she lost it and forgot about it?"). We have coded these questions as a form of socially shared regulation in which students are nominating alternative ideas, but the questions may also function much like Ms. Ramirez's questions. Her contributions initially coregulated the discussion by prompting the students to reveal their thinking to one another and, from a language perspective, by modeling question formation (e.g., "Who do you think is a suspect in this case?"). This combination of coregulation and socially shared regulation, augmented by individual student self-regulation, exemplifies what Merrilyn Goos and colleagues call "collaborative zones of proximal development," in which peers working in small groups "challenged and discarded unhelpful ideas and actively endorsed useful strategies."[6]

Notice also that the causal language students use as their collaboration requires them to argue with evidence for the most plausible answer (e.g., "so" and "'cause"), the conditional sentence constructions (i.e., "What if?") to set up alternative reasoning, and the modal verbs that are required for the conditional mood in English (i.e., "It could have been" and "Why would Annie?").

Throughout this collaborative dialogue, Ms. Ramirez is formatively assessing the students' discipline knowledge, in this case, their reading comprehension. She does not give the students the answer to the whodunit question, but instead asks a series of questions designed to guide their thinking to become more strategic, and to force the students to make a close reading of the text (e.g., "Why do you think that? What page made you think that?"). She also closes with an evaluation that gives them the feedback that they have made "good speculations." Perhaps, with this brief summarization, she is also giving the students a new vocabulary word for what they have been actively engaged in—speculating.

Next, we turn to the transformations that need to occur in classroom practice for self-regulatory processes to flourish.

Transforming Classrooms

We begin this section by outlining the knowledge and skills that teachers need to engage their students in the regulatory processes that we have described throughout this book.

Teacher Knowledge and Skills

1. Teachers need to understand what regulatory processes are, how they contribute to college and career readiness and lifelong learning, and what the processes look like in practice in the classroom.[7]
2. They must also understand formative assessment and have the skills to implement them. They should especially know how to provide feedback that their students can use to move their learning forward and how to embed opportunities for peer feedback and self-assessment into daily classroom practice. Included here are skills in modeling effective feedback and self-assessment—for example, through think-alouds—so that students can adopt what they see and hear around them.
3. Teachers will need to understand the reciprocal relationship between language and self-regulation, socially shared regulation, and coregulation. In other words, they should understand how language can support these regulatory processes and, in turn, how regulation can support language learning. Teachers need the skills to create opportunities for productive interactions between teachers and students and among students and to structure the interactions so that all students have access to the conversations and can contribute in substantive ways. They will also need formative-assessment skills for language learning and must respond to evidence of students' language capabilities to advance students' language competencies. Though these skills are important for all students, they have particular salience for English learners;
4. Also necessary are skills in lesson design that incorporates worthwhile collaborative activity in support of the different forms of regulation. Such designs include tasks that neither impose on learning nor prescribe it, but rather tasks that can be adjusted and shaped by participants because they have initiated regulatory processes.[8]
5. Classroom culture bears strongly on regulatory processes, formative assessment, and language development. Teachers need the skills to model constructive interactions, which, in combination with the participant opportunities the teacher creates, shape the expectations for student

participation in discourse and for a respectful and caring ethos. All students, but especially English learners, need to feel that their contributions are valued by their teacher and peers and will not be subject to ridicule or sanctions.

When teachers have this set of knowledge and skills and implement them effectively, the classroom is transformed into a learner-centered place that promotes self-regulation, socially shared regulation, and coregulation.

How Can Teachers Develop the Necessary Knowledge and Skills?

Teachers need continued professional learning to develop expertise in supporting the various forms of regulation in their classrooms every day. Teacher candidates also need to begin acquiring the knowledge and skills we have just outlined.

The research suggests that professional learning needs to be embedded in the job, collaborative, and sustained; one-shot workshops are far less effective.[9] And just as students need to regulate, so, too, do teachers. They must set their own professional goals, decide how their learning will occur and how they will evaluate its effectiveness, and they need to learn with and from their peers. In this vein, the findings from a recent extensive nationwide survey on the state of teacher professional learning indicate that teachers are not deeply involved in decisions about their own professional learning. Nor, the survey says, are they provided adequate time during the school day to follow up on their professional learning by practicing and applying new skills in the classroom.[10] In what follows, we provide three recommendations for how teachers can be engaged in professional learning to promote regulatory processes in their classrooms.

Recommendations

Leadership support from the school and district plays an essential role in teacher learning. One of the primary reasons that teachers leave the profession is because of inadequate administrative support.[11] Therefore, if teachers are going to be willing to transform their classrooms into environments that promote their students' regulatory processes, they need to be assured of leadership support. This support entails a commitment from schools and districts leaders to numerous aspects of learning regulation: (a) self-regulation, socially shared regulation, and coregulation for students; (b) formative assessment as an integral part of classroom practice; (c) sustained attention to language learning in the content areas for all students and especially for English learners; (d) ongoing professional learning for teachers who can set their own professional goals with support from leaders; (e) adequate time for teachers to learn, plan, and reflect together, ideally not at the end of the school day, when teachers are justifiably tired (US teachers' time spent teaching is higher than the average in Organisation for Economic Co-operation and Development countries); (f) structural changes in schools to enable teachers to work collaboratively; removal of the silos that currently characterize many American schools to make the experience of teaching shared, interactive, and dynamic (teacher surveys consistently show that teachers are more likely to stay in a school that provides a supportive workplace with time for collaboration and professional learning with peers); (g) regular, constructive teacher feedback that is based on evidence of their classroom practice and that will help them advance their skills; (h) opportunities for teacher peers to observe each other's practice with time for debriefing and feedback; and (i) schools and districts that see themselves as enablers of teachers, teaching, and learning and that are willing to acquire the knowledge and skills to develop and maintain a vision of regulated learning for both students and teachers.[12]

We encourage the field to develop and share more rich examples of practice as one way to show both what the integration of these ideas can be like and to illustrate the gap between what *is* happening in many classrooms and what *could* be taking place. We have found in our own work that analyzing videos of practice (the teachers' own practice or the practice of others), along with transcripts of the interactions taking place, is an extremely powerful mechanism for teacher professional learning. After examining their own or others' practice, teachers would also have opportunities to implement ideas that they discussed with their peers and later to reflect on those implementations with their colleagues to further refine those approaches. The goal is not to replicate specific behaviors or actions of other teachers but to identify principles of practice to apply to their own situations, followed by a time to reflect, receive feedback, and revise.

We also encourage the development of protocols that teachers can use for self-assessment or by their peers for observation and feedback. One such example is the *Formative Assessment Rubrics, Reflection and Observation Protocol to Support Professional Reflection and Practice.*[13] This protocol describes the dimensions of formative assessment along a five-point scale, from beginning to extending, and includes tools for teacher to use the scale when they are thinking about their current practice or where to go next. Either through self-assessment or peer observation, teachers work with their peers to determine strategies for moving forward in their practice. Field implementation of this protocol in several states has shown its value in increasing teachers' knowledge and skills about formative assessment and their capacity for classroom implementation. With the strong recommendation for peer learning that we have made, we believe that the development and validation of similar protocols for regulatory processes would be a great benefit to teacher development.

While these recommendations are concerned with teachers who are already qualified and teaching, we also address the need for changes in teacher-candidate programs so that new teachers are fully prepared with the knowledge and skills described above. We advocate disrupting the traditional higher education model of course enrollment in colleges of education and field placement of teacher candidates in classrooms. Instead, we support innovative teacher-preparation approaches that are springing up around the nation. Although they may differ in some of their details, many are situating teacher-candidate programs, along with course offerings, within school systems. In this way, teacher candidates can both learn and work in the field in authentic, sustained, and direct ways with students and classroom teachers throughout most if not all their teaching preparation. For such approaches to work well, teacher candidates must be partnered with high-quality mentor teachers, and these mentorships must be maintained over a period of three or more years once the newly certified teachers are in their own classrooms.[14]

When teachers—and, indeed, teacher candidates—are able to collaborate productively, they can gain pleasure from their joint pursuit and come to appreciate their own as well as their partners' abilities, in the same way that students can do so from their collaborations.[15] We are a case in point. After several years of working and writing together, we deeply appreciate each other's knowledge and skills, we gain immense pleasure from our collaborative efforts, and we are absolutely convinced that the whole is more than the sum of its parts!

Readers of this book will benefit from a summary of what we have learned about students throughout the writing of the book. We will discuss the main characteristics of effective learners and will then summarize additional characteristics that pertain specifically to effective learning by English learners.

Characteristics of Effective Learners

In the list that follows, we present the hallmarks of an effective learner from the standpoint of regulatory processes and language. These student characteristics, culled from the book, provide a succinct profile of the fundamental behaviors and dispositions necessary for students to be effective learners in the classroom. As we have seen with the case examples in this book, teachers can set up a classroom culture (expectations) and use the classroom environment to give students models and strategies to foster the development of these characteristics. Effective learners have the following characteristics or habits:

- Possess all the dispositions we listed in chapter 1.
- Know when and how (linguistically) to use all three regulatory system processes (self-regulation, socially shared regulation, and coregulation).
- Listen carefully to one another, give full attention, and not be distracted or act as a distraction to others.
- Take turns asking and answering one another's questions; this practice requires pragmatic competencies governing communicative behaviors that can be embedded in the routines of the classroom.
- Maintain the focus of the topic, task, or activity at hand (again requires pragmatic competencies).
- Be open to others' ideas and suggestions, and have a disposition that promotes intellectual exchanges.
- Use "invitational" language with others; students know they can foster more frequent and sustained collaborations.
- Are metacognitively aware; they notice similarities and convergences in their own and others' ideas and extend them or transfer them to novel situations.

Even the very youngest learners we have discussed in this book, pre-schoolers Betty and Paola, possess these characteristics, but these hallmarks of effective learning need to nurtured by teachers and peers. With sustained support, these behaviors and dispositions can take root and lead to deeper learning throughout the schooling years and beyond.

What English Learners May Additionally Need

Effective language learners can improve their learning by being self-regulated, regulating the learning of others, and likewise being open to regulation by others when working in collaborative settings. They must also be prepared to learn from others when the regulation of their learning is designed to explicitly assist them in acquiring new language knowledge and skills. Collectively harnessing the potential of the three components of the regulatory system makes students responsible for learning the language. Through such regulation, they can autonomously hone their language skills anytime throughout the school day. Effective learners of language do not wait for the teacher to "give" a language lesson. Rather, they seize every language learning opportunity because these regulatory processes enable them to learn both independently and collaboratively.

In the other direction, students' regulatory processes can be enhanced by their language abilities. With greater linguistic abilities and pragmatic skills, students can, for instance, elicit feedback from a teacher or from their peers more effectively. With greater language acumen, students can also give feedback to others more effectively when working collaboratively. Because the impact of language on regulatory processes, then, is felt in all the content areas of a student's learning, language and regulatory processes are fundamental to the broader academic success of English learners.

English learners may, however, need additional assistance to reach their potential as effective learners. For example, as beginning English learners, they may need language support and nonverbal strategies to join collaborative activities. In addition to the effective learner characteristics listed above, English learners will also need to possess these behaviors or have these dispositions:

- Take risks by "trying on" new language, be it new words, new phrases, or speaking to new people in new situations.
- Move away from the periphery of the conversation (where they may often be physically placed), and communicate by different available means: for example, speaking, writing, gesturing, or drawing.[16]
- Be willing to make mistakes and keep going.

For teachers, the benefits of fostering these English-learner-specific dispositions and the effective learner characteristics could be immense; teachers will have English learner students participating in lessons and collaborative tasks. Fostering these characteristics in shy or reticent but proficient and native-speaking students would also be valuable, of course. But with English learners, teachers and other students will learn unexpected, new perspectives about social science, science, mathematics, and language arts—ideas that they cannot even begin to imagine right now, but which could be valuable contributions rooted in the rich and varied cultures of English learners in their classrooms.[17]

English learner students are already doing a lot to support each other's English and content learning. For example, one group of all newcomer English learners observed by one of us (MH) and her colleagues demonstrated how they supported the collective formulation of a question related to their science class on atoms. The group starts by proposing questions based on what they have observed. Ramiro asks, "Why the particles is around the atom?" Farid follows and asks, "Why this little circle, eh, is smaller and, uh, faster?" Suchada, another member of the group, uses her socially shared regulation abilities to manage the group throughout their exchange, asking, for example, "So which question are you—are we—are we going to ask?" Asef, perhaps the least English proficient student in the group, is able to join in with a motivating "Yeah!" and eventually takes up Ramiro's question himself, repeating, "Why the particles is around the atom?" so every member of the group is actively engaged in the task.[18]

Imagine how, with more proficient English or native English speakers also involved as their group mates in an inclusive classroom, these English learners would be exposed to even more language and discussion of the content they are learning. Their proficient or native English peers in such a situation could support the learners' language through simply conversing with them and by more deliberately coregulating their language and content learning.

Concluding Remarks

In this book, we have explored in some depth the various components of the regulatory system for learning and how teachers can augment their own current classroom practices to support student development in this area and in language learning. We have provided evidence from practice to back our approach to the integration of regulatory processes, language learning, and formative assessment. Future large-scale studies will be necessary to determine more exactly the impact of the approach on students' learning outcomes, changes to teacher practices, and even whether such an approach to teaching and learning will have the lasting societal effects that we believe it will have in terms of equipping students for a fast-changing world.

In the near term, we now invite you to implement the ideas laid out in this book to add to the important practice-based body of evidence. You can manipulate these ideas as necessary for your own classroom to make them work for you or take them one step further by generating and sharing data that can speak to impact at the local level—impact on your teaching and your students' learning.

Notes

Chapter 1

1. Mats Ekholm and Sverker Härd, *Lifelong Learning and Lifewide Learning* (Stockholm: Skolverket [National Agency for Education], 2000); Louise Watson, *Lifelong Learning in Australia* (Canberra: Department of Education, Science and Training, 2003).
2. Natalie L. Bohlmann, Michelle F. Maier, and Natalia Palacios, "Bidirectionality in Self-Regulation and Expressive Vocabulary: Comparisons Between Monolingual and Dual Language Learners in Preschool," *Child Development* 86, no. 4 (2015): 1094–1111.
3. For the impact of language on the self-regulation of students acquiring two languages, see, for example, Gigliana Melzi, Adina R. Schick, and Kelly Escobar, "Early Bilingualism Through the Looking Glass: Latino Preschool Children's Language and Self-Regulation Skills," *Annual Review of Applied Linguistics* 37 (2017): 93–109.
4. Woori Kim and Sylvia Linan-Thompson, "The Effects of Self-Regulation on Science Vocabulary Acquisition of English Language Learners with Learning Difficulties," *Remedial and Special Education* 34, no. 4 (2013): 225–236; Clancy Blair, Alexandra Ursache, Mark Greenberg, and Lynne Vernon-Feagans, "Multiple Aspects of Self-Regulation Uniquely Predict Mathematics but Not Letter-Word Knowledge in the Early Elementary Grades," *Developmental Psychology* 51, no. 4 (2015): 459–472; Megan M. McClelland and Shannon B. Wanless, "Growing Up with Assets and Risks: The Importance of Self-Regulation for Academic Achievement," *Research in Human Development* 9, no. 4 (2012): 278–297; Bohlmann, Maier, and Palacios, "Bidirectionality in Self-Regulation and Expressive Vocabulary."
5. Christopher J. Lonigan, Darcey M. Allan, and Beth M. Phillips, "Examining the Predictive Relations Between Two Aspects of Self-Regulation and Growth in Preschool Children's Early Literacy Skills," *Developmental Psychology* 53, no. 1 (2017): 63–76.
6. Anna Sfard, "Why All This Talk About Talking Classrooms? Theorizing the Relation Between Talking and Learning," in *Socializing Intelligence Through*

Academic Talk and Dialogue, ed. Lauren B. Resnick, Christa S. C. Asterhan, and Sherice N. Clarke (Washington, DC: American Educational Research Association, 2015) 245–254.

7. Christine Howe and Neil Mercer, "Children's Social Development, Peer Interaction and Classroom Learning," *The Primary Review: Interim Reports* (2007): 1–32.

8. Toni Kempler Rogat and Karlyn R. Adams-Wiggins, "Other-Regulation in Collaborative Groups: Implications for Regulation Quality," *Instructional Science* 42, no. 6 (2014): 879–904.

9. See, for example, Monique Boekaerts and Eduardo Cascallar, "How Far Have We Moved Toward the Integration of Theory and Practice in Self-Regulation?," *Educational Psychology Review* 18 (2006): 199–210; Paul R. Pintrich, "A Conceptual Framework for Assessing Motivation and Self-Regulated Learning in College Students," *Educational Psychology Review* 16, no. 4 (2004): 385–407; Barry J. Zimmerman, "Self-Regulated Learning and Academic Achievement: An Overview," *Educational Psychologist* 25, no. 1 (1990): 3–17; Barry K. Zimmerman, "Becoming a Self-Regulated Learner: An Overview," *Theory into Practice* 41, no. 2 (2002): 64–70; Barry J. Zimmerman and Dale H. Schunk, "Self-Regulated Learning and Performance," *The Handbook of Self-Regulation of Learning and Performance*, ed. Barry J. Zimmerman and Dale H. Schunk (New York: Routledge, 2011) 1–15.

10. Zimmerman, "Self-Regulated Learning and Academic Achievement: An Overview"; Zimmerman, "Becoming a Self-Regulated Learner: An Overview."

11. Allyson Fiona Hadwin, Sanna Järvelä, and Mariel Miller, "Self-Regulated, Co-Regulated, and Socially Shared Regulation of Learning," in *The Handbook of Self-Regulation of Learning and Performance*, ed. Barry J. Zimmerman and Dale H. Schunk (New York: Routledge, 2011) 65–84.

12. Lev Semenovich Vygotsky, *Mind in Society* (Cambridge, MA: Harvard University Press, 1978).

13. G. Wells, "Using L1 to Master L2: A Response to Antón and DiCamilla's 'Socio-Cognitive Functions of L1 Collaborative Interaction in the L2 Classroom,'" *Canadian Modern Language Review* 54, no. 3 (1998): 343–353.

14. National Research Council, *Education for Life and Work: Developing Transferable Knowledge and Skills in the 21st Century* (Washington, DC: National Academic Press, 2012).

15. This example comes from a video by Canada's Ministry of Education, Ontario, Canada (used with permission).

16. Linda Allal, "Pedagogy, Didactics and the Co-Regulation of Learning: A Perspective from the French-Language World of Educational Research," *Research Papers in Education* 26 (2011): 332.

17. James G. Greeno, Allan M. Collins, and Lauren B. Resnick, "Cognition and Learning," in *Handbook of Educational Psychology*, ed. David C. Berliner and Robert C. Calfee (New York: Macmillan, 1996), 15–46.

18. Hadwin, Järvelä, and Miller, "Self-Regulated, Co-Regulated."

19. For socially mediated learning, see Vygotsky, *Mind in Society*. See, for example, Neil Mercer, "Neo-Vygotskian Theory and Classroom Education," in *Language Literacy and Learning in Educational Practice: A Reader*, ed. Barry Stierer and Janet Maybin (Clevedon, UK: Open University, 2011) 74–92; Barbara Rogoff, *Apprenticeship in Thinking: Cognitive Development in Social Context* (New York: Oxford University Press, 1990); James V. Wertsch, *Voices of the Mind* (Cambridge, MA: Harvard University Press, 1991).

20. Allyson Hadwin and Mika Oshige, "Self-Regulation, Co-Regulation, and Socially Shared Regulation: Exploring Perspectives of Social in Self-Regulated Learning Theory," *Teachers College Record* 113, no. 2 (2011): 240–264; Sanna Järvelä and Hanna Järvenoja, "Socially Constructed Self-Regulated Learning and Motivation Regulation in Collaborative Learning Groups," *Teachers College Record* 113, no. 2 (2011): 350–374.

21. David Wood, Jerome S. Bruner, and Gail Ross, "The Role of Tutoring in Problem Solving," *Journal of Psychology and Psychiatry* 17, no. 2 (1976): 89–100.

22. Janneke Van de Pol, Monique Volman, and Jos Beishuizen, "Scaffolding in Teacher-Student Interaction: A Decade of Research," *Educational Psychology Review* 22, no. 3 (2010): 271–296.

23. Rogoff, *Apprenticeship in Thinking*, 71.

24. Richard Barwell, "Ambiguity in the Mathematics Classroom," *Language and Education* 19, no. 2 (2005): 118–126.

25. See, for example, Jerome Bruner, *Child's Talk: Learning to Use Language* (Oxford: Oxford University Press, 1985); Rogoff, *Apprenticeship in Thinking*; Catherine E. Snow, "The Theoretical Basis for Relationships Between Language and Literacy in Development," *Journal of Research in Childhood Education* 6, no. 1 (1991): 5–10.

26. Alison L. Bailey, Anna Osipova, and Kimberly Reynolds Kelly, "Language Development," in *Handbook of Educational Psychology*, ed. Lyn Corno and Eric M. Anderman (New York: Routledge, 2015), 202.

27. These approaches include ideas about language developing to serve particular communicative functions (systemic functional linguistics) (e.g., Mary J. Schleppegrell. "Linguistic Features of the Language of Schooling," *Linguistics and Education* 12, no. 4 (2001): 431–59) and language as a complex adaptive system (e.g., Diane Larsen-Freeman, "Chaos/Complexity Science and Second Language Acquisition," *Applied Linguistics* 18, no. 2 (1997): 141–65; Diane Larsen-Freeman and Lynne Cameron, *Complex Systems and Applied Linguistics* [Oxford: Oxford University Press, 2008]; Clay Beckner et al., "Language Is a Complex Adaptive System: Position Paper," *Language Learning* 59, no. s1 (2009): 1–26). This approach conceptualizes language as a "complex nonlinear system" (Larsen-Freeman, "Chaos/Complexity," 157) with interactions between a student's patterns of experience, social interactions, and cognitive processes believed to lead to the emergence of new language structures (Beckner et al., "Language Is a Complex Adaptive System").

28. California Department of Education, *English Language Arts/English Language Development Framework for California Public Schools: Kindergarten Through Grade Twelve (ELA/ELD Framework)* (Sacramento, CA: CDE, 2015).

29. National Research Council, *Education for Life and Work: Developing Transferable Knowledge and Skills in the 21st Century* (Washington, DC: National Academic Press, 2012), 5.

30. Several scholars have referred to "assessment *for* learning." See, for example, Caroline V. Gipp, *Towards a Theory of Educational Assessment* (London: Falmer Press, 1994).

31. Personal communication, cited in Margaret Heritage, *Formative Assessment: A Process of Inquiry and Action* (Cambridge, MA: Harvard Education Press, 2013), 180.

32. Alison Bailey and Margaret Heritage, *Formative Assessment for Literacy, Grades K–6: Building Reading and Academic Language Skills Across the Curriculum* (Thousand Oaks, CA: Corwin Press, 2008); Beverley Bell and Bronwen Cowie, "The Characteristics of Formative Assessment in Science Education," *Science Education* 85 (2000): 536–553; Margaret Heritage, Jinok Kim, Terry Vendlinski, and Joan Herman, "From Evidence to Action: A Seamless Process in Formative Assessment?" *Educational Measurement: Issues and Practice* 28, no. 3 (2009): 24–31; Margaret Heritage, *Formative Assessment and Next-Generation Assessment Systems: Are We Losing An Opportunity?* (Washington, DC: Council of Chief State School Officers, 2010), 1–20; Margaret Heritage, *Formative Assessment: Making It Happen in the Classroom* (Thousand Oaks, CA: Corwin Press, 2010); Harry Torrance and John Pryor, "Developing Formative Assessment in the Classroom: Using Action Research to Explore and Modify Theory," *British Educational Research Journal* 27, no. 5 (2001): 615–631.

33. Paul Black, Chris Harrison, and Clara Lee, *Assessment for Learning: Putting It into Practice* (Maidenhead, UK: McGraw-Hill Education, 2003); Paul Black and Dylan Wiliam, "Assessment and Classroom Learning," *Assessment in Education: Principles, Policy and Practice* 5 (1998): 7–73; Paul Black and Dylan Wiliam, "Developing the Theory of Formative Assessment," *Educational Assessment, Evaluation, and Accountability* 21 (2009): 5–3; D. Royce Sadler, "Formative Assessment and the Design of Instructional Strategies," *Instructional Science* 18 (1989): 119–144.

34. Sue Swaffield, "Getting to the Heart of Authentic Assessment for Learning," *Assessment in Education: Principles, Policy and Practice* 18, no. 4 (2011): 433–449; Torrance and Pryor, "Developing Formative Assessment in the Classroom."

35. Linda Allal, "Assessment and the Regulation of Learning," in *International Encyclopedia of Education,* ed. Penelope Peterson, Eva Baker, and Barry McGaw (Oxford: Elsevier, 2010). 348–352; Black and Wiliam, "Theory of Formative Assessment"; Wynne Harlen, "Formative Classroom Assessment

in Science and Mathematics," in *Formative Classroom Assessment: Theory into Practice*, ed. James H. McMillan (New York: Teachers College Press, 2007), 116–135; Margaret Heritage and John Heritage, "Teacher Questioning: The Epicenter of Instruction and Assessment," *Applied Measurement in Education* 26, no. 3 (2013): 176–190; Brigitte Jordan and Peter Putz, "Assessment as Practice: Notes on Measurement, Tests, and Targets," *Human Organization* 63 (2004): 346–358; Maria Araceli Ruiz-Primo and Erin Marie Furtak, "Informal Formative Assessment and Scientific Inquiry: Exploring Teachers' Practices and Student Learning," *Educational Assessment* 11, no. 3–4 (2006): 237–263; Maria Araceli Ruiz-Primo and Erin Marie Furtak, "Exploring Teachers' Informal Formative Assessment Practices and Students' Understanding in the Context of Scientific Inquiry," *Journal of Educational Research in Scientific Teaching* 44, no. 1 (2007): 57–84. Harry Torrance and John Pryor, *Investigating Formative Assessment* (Buckingham, UK: Open University Press, 1998).

36. Paul Black, Mark Wilson, and Shih-Ying Yao, "Road Maps for Learning: A Guide to the Navigation of Learning Progressions," *Measurement: Interdisciplinary Research and Perspective* 9, no. 2–3 (2011): 71–122.

37. Frederick Erikson, "Some Thoughts on 'Proximal' Formative Assessment of Student Learning," *Yearbook of the National Society for the Study of Education* 106 (2007): 186–216; Heritage, *Formative Assessment: Making It Happen*; Heritage, *Formative Assessment: A Process of Inquiry and Action*; Swaffield, "Getting to the Heart."

38. Lev Semenovich Vygotsky, *Thought and Language* (Cambridge, MA: MIT Press, 1962).

39. Alex Kozulin, Boris Gindis, Vladimir S. Ageyev, and Suzanne M. Miller, eds., *Vygotsky's Educational Theory in Cultural Context* (New York: Cambridge University Press, 2003).

40. Black and Wiliam, "Assessment and Classroom Learning"; John Hattie and Helen Timperley, "The Power of Feedback," *Review of Educational Research* 77 (2007): 81–112; David J. Nicol and Debra Macfarlane-Dick, "Formative Assessment and Self-Regulated Learning: A Model and Seven Principles of Good Feedback Practice," *Studies in Higher Education* 31, no. 2 (2006): 199–218; Sadler, "Formative Assessment and the Design."

41. Hadwin, Järvelä, and Miller, "Self-Regulated, Co-Regulated."

42. Black and Wiliam, "Assessment and Classroom Learning."

43. Zimmerman, "Becoming a Self-Regulated Learner."

44. Avraham N. Kluger and Angelo DeNisi, "The Effects of Feedback Interventions on Performance: A Historical Review, a Meta-Analysis, and a Preliminary Feedback Intervention Theory," *Psychological Bulletin* 119, no. 2 (1996): 254–284. See, for example, Anastasiya A. Lipnevich and Jeffrey K. Smith, "Response to Assessment Feedback: The Effects of Grades, Praise, and Source of Information," *ETS Research Report Series* 1 (2008): 1–57; Hattie

and Timperly, "Power of Feedback"; Valerie J. Shute, "Focus on Formative Feedback," *Review of Educational Research* 78, no. 1 (2008): 153–189.

45. Etienne Wenger, *Communities of Practice: Learning, Meaning, and Identity* (New York: Cambridge University Press, 1998).

46. John Dewey, *The Child and the Curriculum* (Chicago: University of Chicago Press, 1990), 208–209.

47. Greeno, Collins, and Resnick, "Cognition and Learning."

Chapter 2

1. Barry K. Zimmerman, "Becoming a Self-Regulated Learner: An Overview," *Theory into Practice* 41, no. 2 (2002): 64–70.

2. See, for example, Monique Boekaerts and Eduardo Cascallar, "How Far Have We Moved Toward the Integration of Theory and Practice in Self-Regulation?," *Educational Psychology Review* 18 (2006): 199–210; Paul R. Pintrich, "The Role of Goal Orientation in Self-Regulated Learning," *Handbook of Self-Regulation* 451 (2000): 451–502; Paul R. Pintrich, "A Conceptual Framework for Assessing Motivation and Self-Regulated Learning in College Students," *Educational Psychology Review* 16, no. 4 (2004): 385–407; Barry J. Zimmerman and Dale H. Schunk, "Self-Regulated Learning and Performance," in *The Handbook of Self-Regulation of Learning and Performance*, ed. Barry J. Zimmerman and Dale H. Schunk (New York: Routledge, 2011), 1–15.

3. Zimmerman, "Becoming a Self-Regulated Learner."

4. Paul R. Pintrich, "Understanding Self-Regulated Learning," *New Directions for Teaching and Learning* 1995, no. 63 (1995): 3–12; Barry J. Zimmerman and Dale H. Schunk. "Reflections on Theories of Self-Regulated Learning and Academic Achievement," in *Self-Regulated Learning and Academic Achievement: Theoretical Perspectives*, 2nd ed., ed. Barry J. Zimmerman, and Dale H. Schunk (New York: Routledge, 2001): 289–307.

5. Zimmerman and Schunk, "Reflections on Theories."

6. Barry J. Zimmerman, "Self-Efficacy: An Essential Motive to Learn," *Contemporary Educational Psychology* 25, no. 1 (2000): 82–91.

7. Therese Bouffard-Bouchard, Sophie Parent, and Serge Larivee, "Influence of Self-Efficacy on Self-Regulation and Performance Among Junior and Senior High-School Age Students," *International Journal of Behavioral Development* 14, no. 2 (1991): 153–164.

8. Frank Pajares, "Toward a Positive Psychology of Academic Motivation," *Handbook of Positive Psychology in Schools* (2009): 149–160.

9. Zimmerman, "Self-Efficacy: An Essential Motive to Learn."

10. Paul R. Pintrich and Elisabeth DeGroot, "Quantitative and Qualitative Perspectives on Student Motivational Beliefs and Self-Regulated Learning," paper presented at the annual meeting of the American Educational Research Association, Boston, 1990; Scott G. Paris and Alison H. Paris, "Classroom Applications of Research on Self-Regulated Learning," *Educational Psychologist* 36, no. 2 (2001): 89–101.

11. Scott G. Paris and Peter Winograd, "How Metacognition Can Promote Academic Learning and Instruction," *Dimensions of Thinking and Cognitive Instruction* 1 (1990): 15–5.
12. David J. Nicol and Debra Macfarlane-Dick, "Formative Assessment and Self-Regulated Learning: A Model and Seven Principles of Good Feedback Practice," *Studies in Higher Education* 31, no. 2 (2006): 199–218.
13. T. H. Chi et al., "Self-Explanations: How Students Study and Use Examples in Learning to Solve Problems," *Cognitive Science* 13, no. 2 (1989): 145–182.
14. Ann L. Brown, John D. Bransford, Roberta A. Ferrara, and Joseph C. Campione, "Learning, Remembering and Understanding," *Handbook of Child Psychology*, ed. John H. Flavell and Ellen M. Markman (New York: Wiley, 1983): 77–166.
15. David J. Nicol and Debra Macfarlane-Dick, "Rethinking Formative Assessment in Higher Education: A Theoretical Model and Seven Principles of Good Feedback Practice," *Quality Assurance Agency Scotland (Ed.) Reflections on Assessment* 2 (2005): 105–119.
16. Deborah L. Butler and Philip H. Winne, "Feedback and Self-Regulated Learning: A Theoretical Synthesis," *Review of Educational Research* 65, no. 3 (1995): 245–281.
17. D. Royce Sadler, "Formative Assessment and the Design of Instructional Strategies," *Instructional Science* 18 (1989): 121.
18. Ibid., 119–144.
19. James H. McMillan and Jessica Hearn. "Student Self-Assessment: The Key to Stronger Student Motivation and Higher Achievement," *Educational Horizons* 87, no. 1 (2008): 40–49.
20. Paul Black and Dylan Wiliam, "Assessment and Classroom Learning," *Assessment in Education: Principles, Policy and Practice* 5, no. 1 (1998): 7–73; Sadler, "Formative Assessment and the Design."
21. Nicol and Macfarlane-Dick, "Rethinking Formative Assessment," 9.
22. Margaret Heritage, *Formative Assessment: Making It Happen in the Classroom* (Thousand Oaks, CA: Corwin Press, 2010).
23. Pat Turnstall and Caroline Gipps, "'How Does Your Teacher Help You to Make Your Work Better?' Children's Understanding of Formative Assessment," *Curriculum Journal* 7, no. 2 (1996): 185–203.
24. Bronwen Cowie, "Pupil Commentary on Assessment for Learning," *Curriculum Journal* 16, no. 2 (2005):143.
25. Dylan Wiliam, "Formative Assessment: Getting the Focus Right," *Educational Assessment* 11, no. 3–4 (2006): 283–289.
26. Caroline Gipps, "Socio-Cultural Aspects of Assessment," *Review of Research in Education* 24, no. 1 (1999): 355–392.
27. Much of self-regulation remains hidden from view because the processes are mental computations internal to the learner. The same student, for instance, may very well have attempted a very different learning strategy by which he or she uses knowledge of the similarities between some Spanish and English

words. Knowing that Spanish and English words are often cognates (in this instance, words that share the same Latin root in the two languages), the student could have attempted to work out the English equivalent of *seguridad* using a strategy of identifying the systematic sound and spelling patterns across Spanish and English (for example, *g* in Spanish and *c* in English; suffixes that mark the words as nouns: *-dad* and *-ity*). However, in this instance, the student's comparison of the two languages as a learning strategy would have been neither visible nor audible to others. For this book, however, we needed examples of self-regulation that are observable or audible or both, even if fleetingly so, to demonstrate self-regulation. We chose examples from a mix of settings and from as wide a range of examples of self-regulation as possible. We sometimes relied on somewhat artificial situations such as "think-alouds" elicited from students during cognitive labs for assessment development. Such settings expressly ask students to describe their strategies for reading comprehension and problem solving as they are occurring—making external what would otherwise naturally be internal only. On occasion, we have come across classroom video where students are serendipitously speaking aloud as they work on a task (often done deliberately to help them think through a challenging problem). We also have used the interactions found in classroom videos in which students make manifest their self-regulation behaviors when they happen to solicit help from others or describe their self-monitoring practices to their peers or teachers.

28. Mary Lee Barton and Deborah L. Jordan, *Teaching Reading in Science* (Aurora, CO: Mid-continent Research for Education and Learning, 2001), 108.
29. Karl Anders Ericsson and Herbert Alexander Simon, *Protocol Analysis* (Cambridge, MA: MIT Press, 1993); Andrew D. Cohen, "Exploring Strategies in Test Taking: Fine-Tuning Verbal Reports from Respondents," *Learner-Directed Assessment in ESL* (2000): 127–150.
30. Alison L. Bailey et al., "Developing Academic English Language Proficiency Prototypes for 5th Grade Reading: Psychometric and Linguistic Profiles of Tasks," CSE Technical Report 720 (Los Angeles: University of California, National Center for Research on Evaluation, Standards, and Student Testing, CRESST, 2007), http://cresst.org/publications/cresst-publication-3098/sf_s=Bailey.
31. Cohen, "Exploring Strategies in Test Taking"
32. Bailey et al., "Developing Academic English Language Proficiency Prototypes."
33. Video used by permission of the Robert B. Davis Institute for Learning, Rutgers University.
34. Natalie L. Bohlmann, Michelle F. Maier, and Natalia Palacios, "Bidirectionality in Self-Regulation and Expressive Vocabulary: Comparisons Between Monolingual and Dual Language Learners in Preschool," *Child Development* 86, no. 4 (2015): 1,097.

35. For students' ability to use language to support metacognition, see Ray Jackendoff, *A User's Guide to Thought and Meaning* (Oxford: Oxford University Press, 2012).

36. Institute for Learning, University of Pittsburgh. This term was coined by the Institute for Learning to promote rich classroom talk that can support student content learning through the three dimensions of "accountability to the learning community, accountability to accurate knowledge, and accountability to rigorous thinking."

37. Margarita Azmitia, "Expertise, Private Speech, and the Development of Self-Regulation," in *Private Speech: From Social Interaction to Self-Regulation*, ed. Rafael M. Diaz and Laura E. Berk (New York: Psychology Press, 1992): 101–122.

38. Lev Semenovich Vygotsky, *Mind in Society* (Cambridge, MA: Harvard University Press, 1978); Peter Feigenbaum, "Development of the Syntactic and Discourse Structures of Private Speech," in *Private Speech: From Social Interaction to Self-Regulation*, ed. Rafael M. Diaz and Laura E. Berk (New York: Psychology Press, 1992): 181–198.

39. Nancy Eisenberg, Adrienne Sadovsky, and Tracy L. Spinrad, "Associations of Emotion-Related Regulation with Language Skills, Emotion Knowledge, and Academic Outcomes," *New Directions for Child and Adolescent Development* 109 (2005): 109–118.

40. Karen R. Harris, Steve Graham, and Linda H. Mason, "Improving the Writing, Knowledge, and Motivation of Struggling Young Writers: Effects of Self-Regulated Strategy Development With and Without Peer Support," *American Educational Research Journal* 43, no. 2 (2006): 295–340.

41. Zoltán Dörnyei, "Motivation in Second and Foreign Language Learning," *Language Teaching* 31, no. 3 (1998): 117–135.

42. Woori Kim and Sylvia Linan-Thompson, "The Effects of Self-Regulation on Science Vocabulary Acquisition of English Language Learners with Learning Difficulties," *Remedial and Special Education* 34, no. 4 (2013): 225–236.

43. Wen-Ta Tseng, Zoltán Dörnyei, and Norbert Schmitt, "A New Approach to Assessing Strategic Learning: The Case of Self-Regulation in Vocabulary Acquisition," *Applied Linguistics* 27, no. 1 (2006): 78–102.

Chapter 3

1. Nicole C. DiDonato, "Effective Self and Co-Regulation in Collaborative Learning Groups: An Analysis of How Students Regulate Problem Solving of Authentic Interdisciplinary Tasks," *Instructional Science* 41, no. 1 (2013): 25–47.

2. Allyson Fiona Hadwin, Sanna Järvelä, and Mariel Miller, "Self-Regulated, Co-Regulated, and Socially Shared Regulation of Learning," in *The Handbook of Self-Regulation of Learning and Performance*, ed. Barry J. Zimmerman and Dale H. Schunk (New York: Routledge, 2011) 65–84.

3. DiDonato, "Effective Self and Co-Regulation in Collaborative Learning Groups."

4. Shufeng Ma et al., "Children's Productive Use of Academic Vocabulary," *Discourse Processes* 54, no. 1 (2017): 40–61.

5. See, for example, Valeska Grau and David Whitebread, "Self and Social Regulation of Learning During Collaborative Activities in the Classroom: The Interplay of Individual and Group Cognition," *Learning and Instruction* 22, no. 6 (2012): 401–412; Ernesto Panadero and Sanna Järvelä, "Socially Shared Regulation of Learning: A Review," *European Psychologist* 20, no. 3 (2015): 190–203.

6. Marja Vauras et al., "Shared Regulation and Motivation of Collaborating Peers: A Case Analysis," *Psychologia* 46, no. 1 (2003): 19–37.

7. Hadwin et al., "Self-Regulated, Co-Regulated, and Socially Shared."

8. DiDonato, "Effective Self and Co-Regulation in Collaborative Learning Groups."

9. Deanna Kuhn, "Thinking Together and Alone," *Educational Researcher* 44, no. 1 (2015): 46–53.

10. Gary W. Ladd et al., "Grade-School Children's Social Collaborative Skills: Links with Partner Preference and Achievement," *American Educational Research Journal* 51 (2013): 152–183.

11. Kasia Muldner, Rachel Lam, and Michelene T. H. Chi, "Comparing Learning from Observing and from Human Tutoring," *Journal of Educational Psychology* 106, no. 1 (2014): 1–17, cited in Kuhn, "Thinking Together and Alone," 51.

12. Alison L. Bailey and Margaret Heritage, "The Role of Language Learning Progressions in Improved Instruction and Assessment of English Language Learners," *TESOL Quarterly* 48, no. 3 (2014): 480–506.

13. Ma et al., "Children's Productive Use of Academic Vocabulary," 42.

14. Janet Wilde Astington, "Theory of Mind Goes to School," *Educational Leadership* 56, no. 3 (1998): 46–48; Josef Perner, "Theory of Mind," *Developmental Psychology: Achievements and Prospects* (1999): 205–230.

15. Sandra Bosacki and Janet Wilde Astington, "Theory of Mind in Preadolescence: Relations Between Social Understanding and Social Competence," *Social Development* 8, no. 2 (1999): 237–255.

16. Bailey and Heritage, "Language Learning Progressions"; Alison L. Bailey, "Progressions of a New Language: Characterizing Explanation Development for Assessment with Young Language Learners," *Annual Review of Applied Linguistics* 37 (2017).

17. Emily Phillips Galloway, Juliane Stude, and Paola Uccelli, "Adolescents' Metalinguistic Reflections on the Academic Register in Speech and Writing," *Linguistics and Education* 31 (2015): 221–237.

18. David R. Holliway, "Through the Eyes of My Reader: A Strategy for Improving Audience Perspective in Children's Descriptive Writing," *Journal of Research in Childhood Education* 18, no. 4 (2004): 334–349; Marilyn Shatz and

Rochel Gelman, "The Development of Communication Skills: Modifications in the Speech of Young Children As a Function of Listener," *Monographs of the Society for Research in Child Development* (1973): 1–38.

19. Charles A. MacArthur, Shirley S. Schwartz, and Steven Graham, "Effects of a Reciprocal Peer Revision Strategy in Special Education Classrooms," *Learning Disabilities Research and Practice* 6 (1991): 201–210.
20. Linda Allal, "The Co-Regulation of Writing Activities in the Classroom," in Proceedings of the International Conference "de la France au Québec: l'Ecriture dans tous ses états," Poitiers, France, 2008.
21. Ma et al., "Children's Productive Use of Academic Vocabulary," 55
22. Bosacki and Astington, "Theory of Mind in Preadolescence."
23. The example is from the mathematic learning archive of the Robert B. Davis Institute for Learning at Rutgers University (used by permission).
24. Michelene T. H. Chi and Muhsin Menekese, "Dialogue Patterns in Peer Collaboration That Promote Learning," in *Socializing Intelligence Through Academic Talk and Dialogue*, ed. Lauren Resnick, Christa Asterhan, and Sherice Clarke (Washington, DC: AERA, 2015), 265.
25. Ibid.
26. Jennifer Hauver James, Jessica Kobe, and Xiaoying Zhao, "Examining the Role of Trust in Shaping Children's Approaches to Peer Dialogue" *Teachers College Record* 119, no.10 (2017): 1–34.
27. Sarah Michaels and Catherine O'Connor, "Conceptualizing Talk Moves As Tools: Professional Development Approaches for Academically Productive Discussion," in *Socializing Intelligence Through Academic Talk and Dialogue*, ed. Lauren Resnick, Christa Asterhan, and Sherice Clarke (Washington, DC: AERA, 2015) 347–362.
28. Margaret R. Hawkins, "Researching English Language and Literacy Development in Schools," *Educational Researcher* 33, no. 3 (2004): 14–25.
29. Ma et al., "Children's Productive Use of Academic Vocabulary," 55.
30. Filiberto Barajas-Lopez, Noel Enyedy, and Alison L. Bailey, "Language Disconnects Between Small Group Problem Solving and Whole Class Discussions," paper presented at the annual meeting of the American Educational Research Association, Montréal, Québec, April 12, 2005. Used with permission.

Chapter 4

1. Linda Allal, "Pedagogy, Didactics and the Co-Regulation of Learning: A Perspective from the French-Language World of Educational Research," *Research Papers in Education* 26 (2011): 329–336; Nicole C. DiDonato, "Effective Self and Co-Regulation in Collaborative Learning Groups: An Analysis of How Students Regulate Problem Solving of Authentic Interdisciplinary Tasks," *Instructional Science* 41, no. 1 (2013): 25–47; Allyson Hadwin and Mika Oshige, "Self-Regulation, Co-Regulation, and Socially Shared Regulation: Exploring Perspectives of Social in Self-Regulated Learning Theory," *Teachers College Record* 113, no. 2 (2011): 240–264.

2. Allyson Fiona Hadwin, Sanna Järvelä, and Mariel Miller, "Self-Regulated, Co-Regulated, and Socially Shared Regulation of Learning," in *The Handbook of Self-Regulation of Learning and Performance*, ed. Barry J. Zimmerman and Dale H. Schunk (New York: Routledge, 2011) 65–84.

3. Lev Semenovich Vygotsky, *Thought and Language* (Cambridge, MA: MIT Press, 1962).

4. Hadwin and Oshige, "Self-Regulation, Co-Regulation, and Socially Shared Regulation"; Sanna Järvelä and Hanna Järvenoja, "Socially Constructed Self-Regulated Learning and Motivation Regulation in Collaborative Learning Groups," *Teachers College Record* 113, no. 2 (2011): 350–374.

5. Alison King, "Transactive Peer Tutoring: Distributing Cognition and Meta-cognition," *Educational Psychology Review* 10 (1998): 57–74, cited in Marja Vauras et al., "Shared Regulation and Motivation of Collaborating Peers: A Case Analysis," *Psychologia* 46, no. 1 (2003): 19–37.

6. Vauras et al., "Shared Regulation and Motivation"; Lev Semenovich Vygotsky, *Mind in Society* (Cambridge, MA: Harvard University Press, 1978).

7. Toni Kempler Rogat and Karlyn R. Adams-Wiggins, "Other-Regulation in Collaborative Groups: Implications for Regulation Quality," *Instructional Science* 42, no. 6 (2014): 879–904.

8. Hadwin et al., "Self-Regulated, Co-Regulated, and Socially Shared," 68–69.

9. Debra K. Meyer and Julianne C. Turner, "Using Instructional Discourse Analysis to Study the Scaffolding of Student Self-Regulation," *Educational Psychologist* 37, no. 1 (2002): 17–25.

10. Vygotsky, *Mind in Society*.

11. Vauras et al., "Shared Regulation and Motivation."

12. David Wood, Jerome S. Bruner, and Gail Ross, "The Role of Tutoring in Problem Solving," *Journal of Psychology and Psychiatry* 17, no. 2 (1976): 98.

13. Ibid.

14. Janneke Van de Pol, Monique Volman, and Jos Beishuizen, "Scaffolding in Teacher-Student Interaction: A Decade of Research," *Educational Psychology Review* 22, no. 3 (2010): 271–296.

15. Hadwin et al., "Self-Regulated, Co-Regulated, and Socially Shared."

16. Jennie Grammer, Jennifer Coffman, and Peter Ornstein, "The Effect of Teachers' Memory-Relevant Language on Children's Strategy Use and Knowledge," *Child Development*, 84 no. 6 (2013): 1,989–2,002.

17. Ibid., 1,992.

18. Ibid., 1,993.

19. Linda Allal, "The Co-Regulation of Writing Activities in the Classroom," in Proceedings of the International Conference "de la France au Québec: l'Ecriture dans tous ses états," Poitiers, France, 2008.

20. Margaret Heritage, "Assessment for Learning: Co-Regulation *in* and *as* Student-Teacher Interaction," in *Assessment for Learning: Meeting the Challenge of Implementation*, ed. Dany Laveault and Linda Allal (Heidelberg: Springer, 2016).

21. Wood, Bruner, and Ross, "Tutoring in Problem Solving."

22. Vauras et al., "Shared Regulation and Motivation."

23. Sharon Ding and Emma Flynn, "Collaborative Learning: An Underlying Skills Approach," in *Rethinking Collaborative Learning* (London: Free Association Books, 2000), cited in Vauras et al., "Shared Regulation and Motivation."

24. Margaret Heritage and John Heritage, "Teacher Questioning: The Epicenter of Instruction and Assessment," *Applied Measurement in Education* 26, no. 3 (2013): 176–190.

25. See, for example, Alison L. Bailey, "Progressions of a New Language: Characterizing Explanation Development for Assessment with Young Language Learners," *Annual Review of Applied Linguistics* 37 (2017): 241–63; Alison L. Bailey and Margaret Heritage, "The Role of Language Learning Progressions in Improved Instruction and Assessment of English Language Learners," *TESOL Quarterly* 48, no. 3 (2014): 480–506; Alison L. Bailey and Margaret Heritage, "Imperatives for Teacher Education: Findings from Studies of Effective Teaching for English Language Learners," in *A Companion to Research in Teacher Education*, ed. Michael Peters, Bronwen Cowie, and Ian Menter (Berlin: Springer, 2017).

26. Gordon Wells, "Using L1 to Master L2: A Response to Antón and DiCamilla's 'Socio-Cognitive Functions of L1 Collaborative Interaction in the L2 Classroom,'" *Modern Language Journal* 83 no. 2 (1999): 250.

27. Ibid.

Chapter 5

1. Simone Volet, Marja Vauras, and Pekka Salonen, "Self- and Social Regulation in Learning Contexts: An Integrative Perspective," *Educational Psychologist* 44, no. 4 (2009): 215–226.

2. Valeska Grau and David Whitebread, "Self and Social Regulation of Learning During Collaborative Activities in the Classroom: The Interplay of Individual and Group Cognition," *Learning and Instruction* 22, no. 6 (2012): 401–412; Volet et al., "Self- and Social Regulation."

3. National Council of Teachers of Mathematics (NCTM), *Principles to Actions: Ensuring Mathematical Success for All* (Reston, VA: NCTM, 2014).

4. Lorrie A. Shepard, "The Role of Assessment in a Learning Culture," *Educational Researcher* 29, no. 7 (2000): 4–14.

5. Alison Bailey and Margaret Heritage, *Formative Assessment for Literacy, Grades K-6: Building Reading and Academic Language Skills Across the Curriculum* (Thousand Oaks, CA: Corwin Press, 2008). Used with permission.

6. Merrilyn Goos, Peter Galbraith, and Peter Renshaw, "Socially Mediated Metacognition: Creating Collaborative Zones of Proximal Development in Small Group Problem Solving," *Educational Studies in Mathematics* 49, no. 2 (2002): 196.

7. Rebecca Oxford provides several in-depth cameos of second-language learners (predominantly adult) using language learning strategies for listening,

speaking, reading, and writing in everyday contexts, along with recommendations for strategy instruction and assessment by teachers of second-language learners. Rebecca L. Oxford, *Teaching and Researching Language Learning Strategies: Self-Regulation in Context* (New York: Routledge, 2017).

8. Philippe Perrenoud, "From Formative Evaluation to a Controlled Regulation of Learning Processes: Towards a Wider Conceptual Field," *Assessment in Education: Principles, Policy & Practice* 5, no. 1 (1998): 85–102.

9. Linda Darling-Hammond, Maria E. Hyler, and Madelyn Gardner, *Effective Teacher Professional Development* (Palo Alto, CA: Learning Policy Institute, 2017); Michael S. Garet et al., "What Makes Professional Development Effective? Results from a National Sample of Teachers," *American Educational Research Journal* 38, no. 4 (2001): 915–945; William M. Saunders, Claude N. Goldenberg, and Ronald Gallimore, "Increasing Achievement by Focusing Grade-Level Teams on Improving Classroom Learning: A Prospective, Quasi-Experimental Study of Title I Schools," *American Educational Research Journal* 46, no. 4 (2009): 1006–1033.

10. Resources for Learning, "The State of Teacher Professional Learning: Results from a Nationwide Survey" (2017), https://us.corwin.com/sites/default/files/professional_learning_teacher_survey_2017.pdf.

11. Richard Ingersoll, Lisa Merrill, and Daniel Stuckey, "Seven Trends: The Transformation of the Teaching Force," *Consortium for Policy Research in Education* (2014).

12. For the time US teachers spend teaching compared with teachers in Organisation for Economic Co-operation and Development countries, see Centre for Educational Research and Innovation, Organisation for Economic Co-operation and Development, *Education at a Glance 2014: OECD Indicators* (OECD Publishing, 2014), http://dx.doi.org/10.1787/eag-2014-en. For likelihood of teachers to stay in supportive workplaces with time for collaboration and professional learning, see Patte Barth, Naomi Dillon, Jim Hull, and Breanna Holland Higgins, "Fixing the Holes in the Teacher Pipeline: An Overview of Teacher Shortages," Center for Public Education, April 2016, www.centerforpubliceducation.org/Main-Menu/Staffingstudents/An-Overview-of-Teacher-Shortages-At-a-Glance/Overview-of-Teacher-Shortages-Full-Report-PDF.pdf.

13. Caroline Wylie and Christine Lyon, in partnership with the Formative Assessment for Students and Teachers State Collaborative on Assessment and Student Standards (FAST SCASS), *Formative Assessment Rubrics, Reflection and Observation Protocol to Support Professional Reflection and Practice* (Washington, DC: FAST SCASS, 2017).

14. Arthur Levine, *Educating School Teachers* (Princeton, NJ: Education Schools Project, 2006), http://edschools.org/pdf/Educating_Teachers_Report.pdf.

15. Marja Vauras et al., "Shared Regulation and Motivation of Collaborating Peers: A Case Analysis," *Psychologia* 46, no. 1 (2003): 19–37.

16. Margaret R. Hawkins, "Researching English Language and Literacy Development in Schools," *Educational Researcher* 33, no. 3 (2004): 14–25.

17. Alison L. Bailey and Anna V. Osipova, *Children's Multilingual Development and Education: Fostering Linguistic Resources in Home and School Contexts* (Cambridge: Cambridge University Press, 2015); Amelia Wenk Gotwals and Dawnmarie Ezzo, "Formative Assessment: Science and Language with English Language Learners," in *Language, Literacy, and Learning in the STEM Disciplines: How Language Counts for English Learners*, ed. Alison L. Bailey, Carolyn A. Maher, and Louise C. Wilkinson (New York: Routledge, 2018).

18. Margaret Heritage, Aída Walqui, and Robert Linquanti, *English Language Learners and the New Standards: Developing Language, Content Knowledge, and Analytical Practices in the Classroom* (Cambridge, MA: Harvard Education Press, 2015).

Acknowledgments

First and foremost, we thank all the students and teachers whose classroom interactions provided such rich examples of regulatory processes for this book. We are particularly indebted to several superb and generous teachers at the UCLA Lab School and their principal, Norma Silva, for their continuing support of our efforts to increase effective educational practices with English learners everywhere. In particular, we offer our gratitude to Gabriela Cardenas and Olivia Lozano, whose exemplary practice has helped us understand how formative assessment supports regulatory process and language learning. We are also grateful to three teachers from Arizona, Julie Eilertsen, Hilary Johanes, and Jennifer Daniels and their students, whose voices we hear throughout this book. We thank Carolyn Maher, Director of the Robert B. Davis Institute for Learning at Rutgers University, and Noel Enyedy, former Director of Research at CONNECT, UCLA, for their assistance with sourcing classroom videos.

We also thank participants of Alison's graduate seminar for engaging interactions around the first drafts of some of the chapters, especially Qijun Rak Yang for his written comments and Marlen Perez Quintero for her assistance with proofing and reference formatting. Tamara Lau is acknowledged for her excellent graphic work.

Alison also thanks Frank, Nicky, and Will for their unending patience once again. Much of the preparation of this book was done while watching Will play Pony Baseball in the California winter sunshine—can't complain.

Margaret thanks her husband, John, for his unwavering support and encouragement. Finally, our most heartfelt thanks go to Caroline Chauncey at Harvard Education Press, who has been tireless in offering encouragement for the book and providing outstanding feedback along the way—all errors, of course, remain our own.

About the Authors

Alison L. Bailey is Professor of Human Development and Psychology at the University of California, Los Angeles. A graduate of Harvard University, Dr. Bailey is a developmental psycholinguist working on issues germane to children's linguistic, social, and educational development. Her areas of research include first- and second-language acquisition, early literacy development, and academic-language pedagogy and assessment practices with school-age English learners. Her most recent books include *Children's Multilingual Development and Education: Fostering Linguistic Resources in Home and School Contexts* (Cambridge University Press), with Anna Osipova, and *Language, Literacy and Learning in the STEM Disciplines: How Language Counts for English Learners* (Routledge), with Carolyn Maher and Louise Wilkinson. She serves as an advisory board member for numerous states and organizations developing next-generation English language assessments. She is a member of the National Assessment of Educational Progress (NAEP) Standing Committee on Reading (US Department of Education), the National Council on Measurement in Education (NCME) President's Task Force on Classroom Assessment, and the National Academy of Sciences' Consensus Committee on STEM and English Learners.

Margaret Heritage is an independent consultant in education. For her entire career, her work has spanned both research and practice. In addition to spending many years in her native England as a practitioner, a university teacher, and an inspector of schools, she had an extensive period at UCLA, first as principal of the laboratory school of the Graduate School of Education and Information Students and then as an Assistant Director at the National Center for Research on Evaluation, Standards and Student

Testing (CRESST) UCLA. She has also taught in the Departments of Education at UCLA and Stanford. Her current work centers on how formative assessment supports regulatory processes. Her recent books include *English Language Learners and the New Standards: Developing Language Content Knowledge and Analytical Practices in the Classroom* (Harvard Education Press), with Aida Walqui and Robert Linquanti, and *Using Assessment to Enhance Learning, Achievement, and Academic Self-Regulation* (Routledge), with Heidi Andrade.

Index